BY F. F. ROCKWELL
AND ESTHER C. GRAYSON

The Rockwells' Complete Book of Roses
The Complete Book of Bulbs
The Complete Book of Annuals
The Complete Book of Lawns
10,000 Garden Questions Answered (EDITORS)
Gardening Indoors
Flower Arrangement in Color

BY F. F. ROCKWELL

Around the Year in the Garden
The Treasury of American Gardens (WITH JAMES FITCH)
The Book of Bulbs
The Home Garden Handbooks

THE ROCKWELLS'
NEW
COMPLETE BOOK OF
FLOWER ARRANGEMENT

Mrs. T. Bromley Flood

A wall arrangement of roses—winner of the coveted Sterling Silver Bowl Award at the annual nationwide rose arrangement tournament held at Newark, N.J. Blooms carefully selected to show pleasing variation in the development of flowers. Varieties used were Tanya and Golden Chalice.

The Rockwells'

NEW
COMPLETE BOOK
OF
Flower Arrangement

F. F. ROCKWELL

AND

ESTHER C. GRAYSON

WITH 92 FULL COLOR REPRODUCTIONS AND
MORE THAN 150 PHOTOGRAPHS AND DIAGRAMS

AN

American Garden Guild Book

DOUBLEDAY & COMPANY, INC.

GARDEN CITY, NEW YORK

FOREWORD

When, way back in 1935, we wrote our first book on flower arrangement, the publisher hesitated to take it because he felt sure that it dealt with a temporary fad, which in a year or two quite probably would disappear. That book, in several editions, sold some 10,000 copies.

Our second venture, *Flower Arrangement in Color*, five years later, sold 25,000 copies.

The Complete Book of Flower Arrangement, brought out by our present publisher, has run through many printings to reach a total of more than 250,000 in eleven years.

It would seem that the interest in flower arrangement is in no danger of disappearing. On the contrary, and despite its ephemeral nature, it has established itself as a serious art form.

In *The New Complete Book of Flower Arrangement*, we have not merely brought the subject matter of the previous volume up to date but have entirely rewritten and enlarged most of the chapters and added several more. We have—we hope and believe—presented a rather complicated and difficult subject in a way that will make its intricacies readily understandable, even by the beginner. Flower arrangement is an art, and no volume of instructions can create a true artist in any medium unless the inspiration and the capacity to achieve already exist. There are, however, certain general principles that may be presented, and techniques that can be explained. It is in the hope that we are clarifying these principles and techniques for the budding artist that we launch still another volume in this ever-widening—and sometimes tempestuous—sea.

At the launching, we wish to express our thanks to the good friends who have helped make this book possible: to the photographers whose color and black-and-white photographs have preserved the fleeting beauty of the arrangements shown: Frederick W. Cassebeer, noted for his lovely iris as well as for his photographs; Paul Genereux and Gottscho-Schleisner; to Phila Staines and John Burton Brimer for their helpful line drawings and diagrams; and to Faber Birren for the use of several color plates. We would express our appreciation also to the many artists who permitted us to use reproductions of their arrangements; to the many members of the Doubleday staff who have co-operated, with care and often with patience beyond the call of duty, in all the exacting mechanical details involved in designing, correcting and recorrecting color plates, selecting type, and other technical matters involved in completing a volume of this sort.

Finally, we wish to acknowledge gratefully the assistance we found in many of the books by other authors, listed on page 327.

CONTENTS

Part Four

THE PRACTICAL SIDE

ILLUSTRATIONS

FULL COLOR

(By Frederick W. Cassebeer unless otherwise noted)

HALF-TONE ILLUSTRATIONS
(*By Frederick W. Cassebeer unless otherwise noted*)

DRAWINGS AND DIAGRAMS
(By Phila Staines and John Burton Brimer)

INTRODUCTION

When we finished writing the former edition of *The Complete Book of Flower Arrangement* (our third on this particular subject), we threw up our hands in relief, called it a day, and swore we would never again be tempted or persuaded to write another—a pledge we made in good champagne when we "burned the book" in reams of manuscript, galley proofs, and corrected page proofs, inviting our friends in to celebrate the occasion.

Our intentions were good, but resolutions, like soap bubbles, not infrequently blow up in the faces of those who make them. So, because of requests from many friends in the garden world —especially those who had found the original edition useful as a textbook—and the urging of our editors, we agreed to "revise" it.

Did you ever try to revise a ten-year-old perennial garden? You start in with the idea of removing a few old plants, cutting back others, and adding some new ones. You soon become lost in a hopeless tangle, next decide to abandon the entire project, and finally end by digging the whole area up, salvaging the best of what you find, procuring a lot of new material, and making a new border.

Just so, we ended up in this case, not with a revision but with practically a new book, even if it is still in the old area.

HOW TO USE THIS BOOK

A word to new readers on how to get the most help from this volume may be in order. One who is only casually interested in making flower arrangements will gain much, we hope, from even a hasty reading and a study of the many photographs and drawings that illustrate and emphasize the text. In any such hurried perusal of the text it may seem that there is a certain amount of repetition concerning some phases of the subject. This has been done intentionally where it seemed to the authors that it would aid the beginner in getting a clearer picture of the ideas or theories being presented.

To the more serious student of the subject we would make the following suggestions.

First, a reading of the whole book, or at least of all the chapters on theory as well as those covering subjects of special interest to the reader.

Next, a more thorough rereading of all of Part Two (but without paying attention to the suggested exercises) and Chapters 16, 17, 18, and 19 of Part Four.

Finally, a third reading of the above, with careful attention to following up every cross-reference *and carrying out all of the suggested exercises.*

We feel that by following such a course the reader will be assured of getting from these pages what we have tried to put into them and, if planning to be a contestant in the battle for blue ribbons, she will find her chances of success increased.

Have fun—and good hunting!

Part One

FLOWER ARRANGEMENT—
PAST AND PRESENT

1

YOU, TOO, CAN
MAKE ARRANGEMENTS

Perhaps the heading above sounds a bit like a radio commercial or the caption of a colorful advertisement in a woman's home magazine. But it is not—for we have nothing to sell. All we wish to do is try to convince you that, with a very moderate amount of study and practice, you can learn to make flower arrangements that will add immeasurably to the attractiveness of your home surroundings. Moreover, if you so desire and have sufficient patience, you can succeed in capturing prizes at your local flower shows.

We do not wish to convey the impression that every student of this subject can create masterpieces in this comparatively new field of art; new, at least, so far as Western civilization is concerned. (In China, and particularly in Japan, it has been practiced for centuries.) The degree of your success will ultimately depend upon how great a natural flair you may possess for this particular type of self-expression—just as is the case with anyone who takes up music, painting, or sculpture.

The art of flower arrangement is distinct in that even a moderate degree of success, from the very beginning, will be rewarding. And it will be rewarding not only in itself but also in the pleasure it can give to the members of your household and your acquaintances.

On the other hand, we count among our friends many women—and a few men!—who, having taken up flower arranging with considerable doubt as to how successful they

Flowers from the garden, such as day-lilies and lilies, provide material for the beginning flower artist to decorate her home. If she has no garden, or it is out of season, the florist can provide assorted flowers which are not too expensive.

Mrs. Malcolm Russell

would be, have won local or even national reputations in this particular field.

Fortunately for the beginner, the *technique* of arranging flowers can be fairly well mastered in a fraction of the time required in the case of most other arts. It is not essential to devote years of concentrated effort before a reasonable degree of efficiency is attained.

FUN WITH FLOWERS

Therefore, when you begin to give some serious attention to actually arranging your flowers—whether they are from the florist or have been cut in your own garden—you will find yourself, from the very start, having a lot of fun. Instead of merely "sticking them in" any vase, pitcher, or jug that happens to be handy, you will begin to create real designs.

The designs, at first, may be very simple and crude ones. But the very moment you become conscious of attempting to create a design, you will discover a whole new and intensely interesting field opening up before you; and almost without being aware of the effort, you will find yourself selecting blossoms, buds, and sprays of flowers and foliage that can be fitted together, almost like the pieces of a puzzle. The result will be the creation of an arrangement that has definite character and originality—and above all, that is your very own.

Some of these attempts, of course, will please you more than others. At first you may feel that this is merely due to chance. But as you study more extensively, you will find yourself asking "*Why?*" And then finding out why will become a very interesting game indeed.

You will soon discover that in flower arrangement, as in any other art, the whole (that is the ultimate effect created) depends upon a certain relationship of all the parts, or elements, that go to make it up. It soon will become obvious that if any one or more of the parts is not in harmony with the others—is so to speak, a jarring, off-key note—then the effect obtained is less satisfactory than it could be.

As, with practice, you rapidly become more proficient at detecting these "false notes" in your floral compositions, you will almost automatically avoid the repetition of these errors. Your arrangements will be put together with less fussing and effort and turn out to be, when completed, much nearer the ones you visualized in your mind's eye when you began them.

THE FASCINATING CONTAINER GAME

Variety—the spice of life—is also the spice of flower arrangement. It is quite true that a competent arranger can make many different designs in the same vase or other container. The use of a number of containers, however, multiplies manyfold the effects that may be achieved. Certain arrangements demand containers of certain types. It would be quite impossible, for instance, to do any arrangement similar to that shown on page 32 in the container shown on page 37. Thus the beginning arranger will not have progressed far before realizing that the possession of at least a moderate assortment of containers is absolutely essential. This, in turn, opens up a fascinating hobby associated with that of arranging. Even the most casual scanning of the photographs in these pages will show how important a part the container can play in the creation of lovely and out-of-the-ordinary floral compositions. Often the design of the container suggests the motif for the arrangement itself, a motif which otherwise would never have occurred to the artist.

Whether or not the acquisition of interesting containers becomes a real hobby, you are sure to get a thrill out of hunting up and procuring a few of them. The game need not be an expensive one, and it can add immeasurably to the pleasure you find in flower arranging. If hubby happens to have the "do-it-yourself" malady, he may like to turn out some original containers, bases, or accessories for you. This, naturally, may have its dangerous aspects. You alone can judge as to this possibility.

GROWING FOR ARRANGING

There are thousands of arrangers, and many of them very expert ones, too, who never grow flowers of their own. It seems to us, however, that the greatest pleasure to be had from arranging flowers comes only when one can grow the materials used, or at least a goodly part of them. Conversely, no matter how successful one may be in growing flowers, we find the most complete satisfaction from them is to be had only when, after they are grown, they can be shown in such a way as to display both their individual beauty and their merit as material in the creation of lovely designs. Such arrangements as those reproduced on pages 24, and 44 well illustrate this dual role.

However, the greatest advantage of growing your own flowers is that you can have them in assortment, not only of variety and color but also in the degree to which they have developed. It is infinitely more difficult to construct a pleasing arrangement without an assortment of buds, half-opened flowers, and full-blown blossoms.

When you buy flowers from the florist, they come as nearly exactly alike as peas in a pod; or it might be more accurate to say like peas compressed into a frozen cellophane pack. A dozen florist's roses, carnations, or snapdragons are usually all of the same color, with stems all the same length and all open to the same degree. And of course the longer and bigger and stiffer the *stems*, the more you pay for the flowers! Supplementary foliage, if any, is likely to consist of a token spray or two of "asparagus," huckleberry, Christmas fern, or lemon.

I recall with amusement an experience I once had at the city apartment of a very fine lady whose birthday was being celebrated. The living room was done, but not overdone, in a rather grand manner, with some fine pieces of old furniture, paintings that must have cost a small fortune, and hangings chosen in excellent taste. The only jarring note was the flowers

—beautiful specimens sent by admiring friends and stuck, as best they could be, at all angles, in any bowls or vases that were large enough to hold them.

I think our hostess must have noticed something in my expression as I viewed them. She said: "They do look awkward, do they not? What is wrong with them? I hear you have written a book about arranging flowers. Can't you do something with these?"

Saying that I would not think of disturbing them, I tried to beg off, but she was persistent. So finally I countered with, "Well, if you insist, but only under three conditions. First, a warning that you are going to be terribly shocked at what I do to them—and of course you will not be able to restore them to their present appearance any more than you could put Humpty Dumpty together again. Second, that I have a free hand to do as I please. Third, that I can make use of any other containers you have available."

For a moment I thought I had got the better of the situation; but she caught her breath, looked grim, and finally said, "It's a deal"—and rang for her maid.

On the maid's arrival, she said, "Please show this gentleman the closet where we keep the bowls and vases and get him any he asks for."

We found several very interesting copper containers and also reclaimed the remains of some autumn foliage on its way to the trash can. When I started to cut off and discard a total of two thirds of some of the beautiful long, stiff stems of the flowers, there were smothered but quite audible expressions of dismay about the room. By blowing some blooms wide open and compressing others, it was possible to get at least a little difference in shape and size. And the remnants of the autumn foliage we had picked up helped considerably.

The resulting on-the-spot "arrangements," as might be expected, were nothing to be proud of, especially as there were no holders of any kind available. The effect, however, when they had been placed in advantageous locations, was interesting and arresting. If, under the watchful eyes of the little assembly,

I had taken a dozen Easter eggs and a setting hen out of the tiny beaded bag that lay on a table near me, the expressions of surprise could not have been greater. The surprise on my part lay in the fact that here was a group of women, each one of whom undoubtedly prided herself either on her artistic abilities or at least her taste, completely astonished at the change a few flower arrangements, of very mediocre quality, could make in the general appearance of that room.

YES, YOU, TOO, CAN ARRANGE FLOWERS

Let us repeat that *you* can learn the rewarding art of arranging flowers. There is nothing mysterious about it, and it will require no technique that will necessitate years of training or any special skill.

Even if you lack the artistic sense of designing in form and color which comes naturally to some individuals, you can still learn to make arrangements that will give a great amount of pleasure to both yourself and those around you. Your home will be more colorful and cheerful, and you will find happiness in a new form of self-expression.

Your progress in this rewarding home art will be most rapid if you take the time to study some of the arrangements made by those who have become proficient at it and learn to analyze the several factors which make certain arrangements particularly pleasing and others only so-so. But first let's take just a few minutes to glance at the origin of flower arrangement as an art and its development down through the years to the present time.

2

FLOWER ARRANGEMENTS
OF THE PAST

Since the beginning of recorded time, and probably long before, flowers have been used to adorn the habitations of man and to play an important part in his feasts, celebrations, and religious rituals.

It is only recently, however, that "flower arrangement," in the sense which that phrase now implies, has been a conscious art in the Western world. In the East, Japan alone developed the use of flowers and foliage in decorative designs into anything which might be termed an art. And to the Japanese we must frankly give credit for the influence which, more than any other, has made our modern flower art what it is today.

In later chapters of this book may be found accounts in some detail of the practices followed in the use of flowers during past eras. What we are concerned with here is merely a glance at what was done in each era and the part it played in the culture associated with it.

First of all, we must face the fact that from past centuries few records remain of the actual use of cut flowers. To gain an insight into their use, we must look to the interior decoration of each age, to its horticultural history, textile designs, architectural motifs, and—most of all—to the still lifes and paintings by the artists of each period, which include cut-flower material. From these sources we can piece together the floral fashions of the past.

CHINA—In China, cut flowers may have been used, to our knowledge, since 618 A.D. when they were offered on the altars in Buddhist temples. During the Sung Dynasty, 960 to 1280 A.D., the late Ming Dynasty, 1368 to 1644 A.D., and the Ch'ing Dynasty, 1644 to 1912, paintings and other works of art show that floral decoration played an important part in peacetime culture. Today in China, as in the past, plant material is used symbolically for seasonal decoration, celebrations, holidays, and for personal greetings and congratulations.

JAPAN—In Japan, flower arrangement has been an art since the sixth century A.D. when it was brought there from China by missionary Buddhist priests. Its evolution since then has been constant but varied. In all phases it has been characterized by highly stylized schools, led by master teachers, each with rigid rules in regard to material to be used, its manner of use, and even the containers in which it may be arranged.

Flower arrangement has always been and still is a vital part of Japanese culture. It has its place in even the humblest home, as well as in the most luxurious, and is still used in the tea ceremony and other social rituals.

During World War II, Japanese Americans interned on the West Coast beautified their crude quarters, to make their internment more bearable, by the exquisite compositions which they made of the most unpromising materials—stones, wood, and the few bits of living plant material available.

We have heard it said that, in deserted Japanese military barracks captured by our forces late in the war, flower arrangements were often found, still standing on the window sills of the soldiers' sleeping quarters. No wonder our own modern flower art owes much to the inspiration and example of the Japanese.

BYZANTIUM—Floral art in the ancient civilizations of the Near East is perhaps best exemplified by that of Byzantium, the eastern capital of the Roman Empire, which survived for centuries after the fall of Rome itself.

Here formal, symmetrical cones and pyramids, classic wreaths and garlands of foliage, fruits, and flowers reached a rigid, studied perfection all its own, though of Greek inspira-

A typical "period" arrangement showing Flemish influence, in which a great many flowers have been crowded together in opulent confusion, but with little attention to creating an interesting design. (Compare with the arrangement on page 41.)

tion. Many of the formal, symmetrical, massed modern arrangements of today stem back to these roots.

RENAISSANCE—In Europe, after the sterile lag of creative inspiration during the Dark Ages, the Renaissance brought distinctive and characteristic forms of floral art in keeping with the décor of the times.

For a better insight into European flower art from 1400 to the early twentieth century, see Chapter 11, in which are discussed the Renaissance, Baroque, Rococo, Classical Revival, Romantic, French Impressionist, and Art Neuveau periods of art and decoration. This span of time represents wide swings of the pendulum from great artificiality, elaborate and ornate, to severe classicism, and then back through the Romantic period to naturalism.

GEORGIAN—In England the Georgian period was characterized by vigorous, massive floral and fruit compositions which reflected the art influences of France, Italy, and the Orient. Englishmen had begun to travel widely throughout the world, and from their voyages they brought back the décors of other countries to incorporate into their own culture.

CLASSIC REVIVAL—Following this period in England, Neoclassicism overtook the Western world, crowding out the remnants of elaborate Baroque and Rococo taste and substituting instead the straight, classic symmetry epitomized by the Directoire and Empire periods in France, Regency in England, Biedermeier in Germany, and the Greek Revival on this side of the Atlantic.

In floral decoration this trend expressed itself in classic urns of fruits and flowers, symmetrical in design, and in a revival of the use of garlands, wreaths, and flower-filled scarves, a natural reaction to the massed profusion of decoration in the periods immediately preceding.

VICTORIAN—It was quite natural, too, that the years of classic severity in decoration should be followed by revolt. In England this expressed itself in the long, fussy, overelaborate, "tasteless" (to our modern eyes) décor of the reign of Queen Victoria. Not until her death and the coming of Art Nouveau at the end of the nineteenth and the beginning of the twentieth centuries were the British and—to a large extent—the Americans freed of this stultifying influence.

AMERICA—In America, interior decoration was naturally less influenced by European styles, especially during the early years of settlement and colonization.

The rigors of life in early New England, combined with the unbending religious prejudices of the people, must have left little time or opportunity for interior decoration with cut flowers. We know, however, that the settlers brought roots and seeds, cherishing these in their gardens. Whether or not cut flowers were permitted indoors we really do not know; but if so, they must have been few and placed in utilitarian containers.

In the wealthier colonies of Virginia, Maryland, New York, and Pennsylvania, on the other hand, objects of art had been imported before 1700, and the finer houses and plantations could boast elegant containers of many kinds in which to arrange flowers.

During the first three quarters of the eighteenth century, a great variety of plant material and decorative art objects came to the New World; and as more gracious living became possible toward the close of the century, echoes of Europe's Classic Revival reached our shores.

In the nineteenth century, Victorian influence permeated American décor, until—from 1890 to 1910—Art Nouveau took over with its fresh, original designs and materials, such as were exemplified in Tiffany glass.

Gradually these earlier modes merged into the present period of modern décor, with its highly developed art of flower arrangement characterized by well-designed containers in neutral colors, rhythmic or geometric in form. Although flower designs are highly stylized, a variety of styles are used, always employing recognized color harmonies.

3

PRESENT-DAY
FLOWER ARRANGEMENTS

When we wrote our first book on flower arrangement (back in 1935), the use of flowers displayed in artistic designs, or "arrangements," instead of merely as horticultural specimens or as bouquets, was just beginning to become a prominent feature at some of the larger flower shows. This new art—new at least to the Western world—caught on like a fire in a California forest.

Within a few years the "arrangement classes" became the leading feature in any show or section of a show in which women had a part and even made inroads into such specimen-dominated one-flower shows as those of the dahlia and gladiolus societies.

It is difficult to realize today how deep, in some quarters, was the resentment against the invasion of the arrangers. A dahlia society to which I belonged and which, quite characteristically, held its meetings in the back room of a barber shop, was split in two because the real, dyed-in-the-wool dahlia fans refused to permit the showing of any other flowers —or even of dahlias themselves—in arrangements in the club's annual show. In such shows, incidentally, a very essential part of the equipment of every judge was a pocket rule to measure the diameter and depth of each bloom!

What a difference today. Now every woman with any pretension at all to the social amenities knows what flower arrangement is, and probably will have tried her hand at it,

Mrs. Loren R. Dodson

Mrs. Tom Cummings

PAST AND PRESENT. *Above are a mass composition of the Flemish period and a Japanese line arrangement—the two extremes of Occidental versus Oriental ideas concerning flower art. Below are their contemporary prototypes, a modern mass and a modern line-mass arrangement, each of which shows evidence of influence from both sources.*

Mrs. William Joy

Mrs. Anne Elizabeth Erhorn

A modern line-mass arrangement using but one kind of flower, with harmonizing supplementary foliage.

even if in an untutored and amateurish way. Now the arrangement classes at the smallest flower shows, as well as the larger ones, are the principal center of attention.

Throngs wait for the judging—and a very serious business it is, indeed!—to be concluded, and then crowd in to see to whom and to what the awards have been given. And as anyone keeping an ear open will soon discover, there is no hesitation about criticizing the decisions that have been made. Many of these criticisms, of course, are without foundation and show only ignorance on the part of those who have made them. A surprising number of such comments, however, are well taken and occasionally well merited.

To the members of women's garden clubs must go most of the credit for this tremendous growth of interest in flower arrangement. Especially is credit due to those in the upper echelons of the Federated Garden Clubs of America and The Garden Club of America—the latter perhaps as much noted for its blue stockings as its blue ribbons but, nevertheless, a very potent factor in advancing the status of flower arrangement. Both of these groups have done yeoman service in the cause of American horticulture in general, with outstanding educational exhibits at leading flower shows and many excellent publications. Probably the most effective factors in advancing flower arrangement in this country, we believe, have been the yearbooks and other publications of the National Council of State Garden Clubs, as well as their development of judging schools and trained "accredited" judges. Occasionally, in our opinion, they have gone overboard in emphasizing *rules* to be followed in making and judging arrangements—but of that more in a later chapter.

If further proof were needed as to the tremendously increased interest in flower arranging, it could be found in the fact that lectures and demonstrations on the subject are now frequently broadcasted on radio and television. In fact the most dramatic (and most highly paid) author and lecturer in this field was recently sponsored by one of the largest users of air space, and in color.

PRESENT TRENDS

Popular fads come quickly, and as quickly fade into innocuous desuetude. Flower arrangement does not belong in the category of fads: it is no hula-hoop proposition capturing overnight the fancy of the multitudes for a few weeks or months and then passing into oblivion.

It has now been steadily gaining in popularity for several decades and shows every indication of continuing to do so. Even the commercial florists—who as a rule are about as slow to adopt new ideas as any group we know of—have begun to pay some attention to it and now conduct their own arrangement schools and competitions. It is true that the old standard set pieces—such as "gates ajar," "broken columns," and funeral "pillows," made on manufactured wire frames stuffed with sphagnum moss—have passed into limbo and in their place are appearing decorations which show some signs of beauty and originality. The really creditable ones, however, are still woefully few. Nevertheless, the top annual award made by the New York Florists' Club, one of the largest in the country, has several times gone to a good friend of ours who is a partner in a small florist shop in a commuting area near Manhattan. Her designs have originality and beauty and are really good arrangements. All this indicates some progress on the part of the judging committee at least.

To get the greatest pleasure from your flowers, however, even if you must buy them instead of growing your own, you will wish to arrange them yourself. So that brings us back to our current theme, the *art* of arranging flowers.

As with other arts, that of arranging is not static. It progresses; it changes with changing times; it has its periods and its "schools." What is modern today becomes antiquated tomorrow and by the day after is obsolescent—just as happens with painting, music, or poetry. If your heart is set on winning blue ribbons at flower shows, you will have to pay attention to these trends, trends which we shall attempt to explain and explore in later chapters of this book.

It has always seemed to us, however, that the greatest pleasure to be had in this interesting field lies in the artistic use of flowers for home decoration, rather than in creating masterpieces—in the mode of the moment, of course—that will add to the ribbon collection. The literary department of your woman's club may insist, and quite rightly so, on reading of such moderns as T. S. Eliot, Dylan Thomas, and Boris Pasternak, but that need not keep you from enjoying an evening by the fireside with a book of Shelley, James Stephens, or Edna St. Vincent Millay. As in other arts, arrangements which are well designed are worthy of admiration whether or not they are in the current fashion. We study, and sometimes copy, the rich floral paintings of the old Flemish masters though they are no longer in the current mode.

So what we like to term contemporary flower art is not a static thing. Like most of the arts, it shifts and changes more rapidly today than ever before in history. It is not to be tied down by rules and regulations. Also, like the other arts, it is founded upon certain principles of design which are permanent —at least for the foreseeable future—and which must be understood by the artist who has a desire to do really good work. The road to a real knowledge of these principles is a much longer and steeper one than that traveled by the imitator or copyist. We say that an author's work is "derivative" when the discerning reader can see from what other writers he has derived his style and method. Many arrangers copy what they see in other shows or in books on arrangement, but they will never become first-rate artists by following this method. There is infinitely more satisfaction in studying the principles and techniques in order to create compositions of originalty and distinction.

A typical show arrangement in the modern mode, with flowers playing a minor role but with meticulous attention to design, color, and texture.

4

ARRANGEMENTS FOR THE HOME
AND FOR SHOWING

Before discussing the techniques of arranging flowers, it may be well to consider the difference between making flower compositions that are created primarily to add beauty and brightness to our daily lives and those that are designed for exhibition to win awards in flower-show competition.

We feel very strongly that in most of the books and articles on flower arrangement, excellent as many of them are, entirely too much emphasis has been placed on the exhibition type as compared to the everyday "enjoy-it-at-home" type.

As far as we are aware, the New York *Times*, in its garden pages—of which one of your authors was then editor—was the first publication to pay serious attention to this new phase of, or adjunct to, gardening. The crowds pressing around the arrangement section in any big show made it evident that the public found this new art to its liking. The inevitable result was that those who had an inborn flare for arranging soon found themselves "authorities" on the subject and much in demand as lecturers and teachers. Quite naturally, but unfortunately, too much emphasis was laid upon the type of arrangement that might be expected to win awards at flower shows, and not enough upon the general principles of composition that apply to all creative arts. This led to quite rigid "rules" as to what was desirable, or even permissible, in the making of arrangements; and consequently the art of arrangement still suffers, though not so much as formerly, from this one-sided emphasis.

Let us see if we can discover just what does make a flower arrangement tick: what factors cause us to consider it a good arrangement, or a poor one.

The beginning arranger, when she starts to exhibit, soon learns that the majority of judges, getting their training in schools or classes for judging—as they must before being officially recognized as accredited judges—will look for and approve certain things in an arrangement because they follow the rules; and consider others, regardless of their basic artistic merit, objectionable just because they are exceptions to the rules.

It is quite true—and certainly we would be the last to deny it—that competitive exhibitions of arrangements at flower shows have been the most effective of all forces in developing flower arrangement in this country; but if that development is to continue, both arrangers *and judges* must be on guard against any tendency to freeze this comparatively new art into a prescribed set of patterns.

ARRANGEMENTS FOR THE HOME

The making of arrangements for home decoration should be a joyous occupation, freely indulged in. There need be no worry about what the judges might think of them. Too much striving for what may be termed "flower-show perfection" will take much of the enjoyment out of what should be a more or less spontaneous expression of such artistic capabilities as the arranger may possess.

In our own case, not a day goes by during spring, summer, and autumn that does not bring some new experiment in combining flowers and foliage to decorate a mantel, a table top, a desk, a shelf, or a bureau. Many of these require not more than ten or twenty minutes in the making. There is no attempt to make them conform to flower-show rules. There is an endeavor, of course, to follow the general principles of good design (as presented later in this volume) but the attainment

Miss Mildred Sawyer

Two arrangements for the home. Above, a handful of daffodils (Poeticus type) in a cake dish; below, petunias in a simple design.

Esther C. Grayson

Mrs. Eleanor Towne Carey, Jr.

For a console table in the home, with a portrait hanging on the wall above, a simple arrangement of pine and anemones enhances the picture. Fruit and hurricane lamp provide balance. For a table against a neutral wall, spring flowers lend a bright, colorful note.

Mrs. Arthur N. Peck

of perfection is not the principal objective. As a part of our everyday living, we are much more interested in *flowers* than we are in arrangements.

"Why then," someone may ask, "bother to arrange them at all? Why not just gather them into an old-fashioned bouquet and put them in a bowl?" The answer is that one cannot intimately enjoy flowers en masse any more than one can expect to enjoy, at a cocktail party, an intimate conversation with a friend. Even in those very massive arrangements of the old Dutch painters, the individual blooms stand out quite distinctly, often in marvelous detail. The reason for this, of course, is that such compositions follow the principles of design.

The practice of making "quickies" for home decoration will prove of great value even to those who are primarily interested in making show arrangements. The old adage that "practice makes perfect" applies here as elsewhere. The more familiar one becomes with the mechanics of flower arranging, the more facility is acquired in making flowers and foliage behave as one wishes them to and stay put in their assigned positions. In fact it is only when such techniques have been acquired to the point where they require little conscious attention that there is much hope of one's becoming a consistent ribbon winner in flower-show competition.

ARRANGEMENTS FOR SHOWING

Flower arrangers are of two quite distinct types: those who take it up for the fun of the thing and the pleasure of artistic creation and those, by nature more competitive, to whom the accomplishment of *winning* is the greatest reward. Which of these two groups you may belong to has probably been determined by the particular genes handed down to you through many generations of ancestors. If you belong to the second, your chances of becoming a consistent ribbon capturer are greater, but you will probably have less fun along the way.

Some of the most bitter personal feuds we have ever observed have been between persons belonging to the latter group. It has caused us some amusement to observe them from the side lines—even when, occasionally, we have had, figuratively speaking, to dodge a stray flower holder or two.

Flower arrangement in this country has developed into a genuine art. Any person who plans to take it up at all seriously should realize this fact and be prepared to study religiously and devote to it a worth-while period of apprenticeship. There are, of course, just as in any art, those who are so fortunate as to possess a natural flair for it and whose progress will be rapid.

Flower arrangement does have the advantage that necessary mechanical techniques may be mastered in a fraction of the time required in the same field in most other arts, such as music or painting. Mastered they must be, however, before one becomes really proficient, and this will take time and serious application.

Another advantage is that, almost from the very start, you will be able to make arrangements that will have some merit and be infinitely better than you could have made without a study of the subject. Gradually you will begin to realize how much even passably good arrangements, well placed, can add to the cheerfulness of your home.

You will then be ready for the novice classes in shows, and as these yield blue ribbons, you automatically move up into more difficult and complicated competitive classes where real talent and skill may yield the honors you are seeking.

Part Two

THE ART OF ARRANGING FLOWERS

5

JUST WHAT IS A FLOWER
ARRANGEMENT?

Before one sets about making a flower arrangement, it is essential to have a mental picture of just what constitutes an "arrangement," or a "floral composition." In this chapter and the following ones on *theory*, the two terms above are used interchangeably. For their more specific definitions, as employed in competitive classes in flower shows under the rules of the Federated Garden Clubs, see page 248. At this point we are interested in how an arrangement or floral composition differs from a mere bouquet or a bowlful of flowers.

An exact definition is difficult. Perhaps the best answer is to say that an arrangement is a *planned* composition, while a bouquet is not. The flowers in one may be the same as those in the other. The difference lies in the way they are placed *in relation to each other*.

In a bouquet it makes little difference how the flowers are placed; but when we attempt to arrange them to form a composition, they at once become subject to certain principles that apply to any composition in any art medium—to a painting, an etching, a piece of sculpture, or a musical composition.

Look about you. The room in which you are sitting, if it is well arranged, offers many examples of compositions of various sorts. The pictures on the wall have not been placed haphazardly; the chairs and tables are set in relation to wall areas and to each other; the decorations on the mantel above the fireplace, even the utilitarian fire tools beside it, have been given careful thought as to their placement. The result is that

Mrs. George Goldson. First Prize

A careful study of this bold and apparently simple arrangement will show that it follows all of the basic principles of design: unity, scale, accent; and balance, harmony, and rhythm. Pick them out and study them one by one.

the room as a whole is a planned composition; how good or how poor a composition depends upon the taste and skill of the one who arranged it and the suitability of the materials that were available to work with.

DESIGN COMES FIRST

Take another look about the room at the different objects in it: the windows, the walls, the fireplace, the chairs, the table, and the lamp upon the table. Each and every one of these

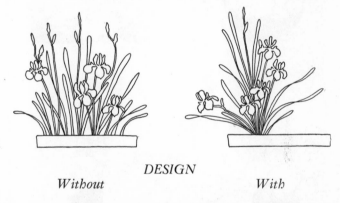

DESIGN

Without   *With*

represents a design; each is the material manifestation of a mental picture in the mind's eye of the designer, a picture that existed, that had to exist, before it could become a reality in wood or plaster, brick or stone, paint or metal. Each of these objects—no matter how widely they may vary in form, color, or texture—possesses one thing in common with all the others: it has *oneness*. It is a unit every part of which is subservient to the whole and is employed, in its relationship to all the other parts, to combine with them to make the whole.

Now you can comprehend what John Ruskin, one of the world's greatest teachers of art and art appreciation, meant when he wrote that the great object of composition is "always to secure unity—that is to make things whole. The first mode in which this can be effected is by determining that one feature shall be more important than all the rest, and that others shall group with it in subordinate positions."

So with your flower arrangements, the design must exist first in your mind's eye, as a single unit, before you begin to transform it into material existence.

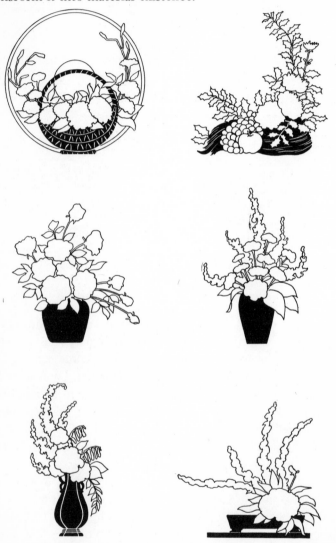

The container should be selected to harmonize with the over-all design.

Design may be good, bad, or indifferent, but it is still design. A design that strikes one observer as being good may not appeal to another. To the admirer of modern art, for instance, the designs in a composition by Picasso may seem the acme of perfection, whereas to one who admires such works as those of Corot or Bonheur, it may seem the exact opposite; but the admirer of either type of composition will still admit that the other possesses design.

Design is the form, or shape of the composition—the thought-out plan upon which it is built. If you take a careful look at any of the arrangements reproduced in this book, one thing must strongly impress you: none of them could have "just happened." In each instance there is a *planned* relationship between all the component parts: between the various flowers, the foliage, between both of these and the container which holds them. These relationships are called the basic principles of design. To qualify as being of acceptable design, the composition must possess:

> Unity
> Scale
> Accent (a focal point and center of interest)

To be of really good design—one which pleases the eye and satisfies the esthetic taste of the beholder—the composition must further possess:

> Balance
> Harmony
> Rhythm

THE THREE BASIC PRINCIPLES

Let us first consider *Unity*, *Scale*, and *Accent*, the three which are most essential because, without *all* of them, we would have merely a chaotic jumble of unrelated parts instead of a design.

Mrs. L. N. Wilson, Mrs. Robert D. Veghte, and Mrs. Constance B. Wallace

UNITY: The first principle of design is unity. The arrangement as a whole must be a unit: each part (or element) in it must be so related to every other part that the result is oneness. Whatever the materials used—flowers, foliage, container, base, accessories—no matter how few or how many, they must blend to make a unified whole.

Mrs. Tom Cummings

SCALE: *If the design is to be a good one, its several parts—the materials used in constructing it, the container, the accessories— must possess a suitable relationship to each other in size. A group of smaller flowers or leaves may serve as a unit which will be in scale with larger individual leaves or blooms used in the design, as in the arrangement on page 58.*

Mrs. J. C. Graham

ACCENT: *Accent, visual center of interest or focal point, is essential in good design. In the arrangement above, it is accomplished by the placement of the two wide-open roses at the center of the design. This bull's eye effect is further heightened by the forms and stem lines of the smaller roses above, and by the grape-hyacinths, chionodoxas, lilies-of-the-valley, and ivy leaves which lead the eye to them. Other methods of creating accent are described on pages 63 to 64.*

Mrs. H. T. Langworthy

BALANCE: *In a flower arrangement, equilibrium is a matter of* visual *balance rather than the actual physical weights of the materials used. In general, the visual weight of all the materials on one side of an imaginary vertical line extending up through the container and materials should be approximately the same as on the opposite side. This is true of both symmetrical and asymmetrical balance.*

Mrs. A. W. Jennings

HARMONY is a more subtle quality in an arrangement than any
of those principles previously discussed. In the arrangement above,
it is expressed by both the form and the texture of the base, the
accessory, and the materials employed. The blunted head and tail
of the prehistoric reptile find a perfect foil in the pointed leaves and
buds of the plant material while the textures are ingeniously
matched throughout.

Mrs. Claire Stickles

RHYTHM *in a composition of any kind is that quality which gives it a sense of motion—a feeling created by the actual movement of the eye as it follows the curving line of the crescent in the arrangement above, to and through the center of interest, and then back again. (Just pinpoint your gaze on any one spot in this curve and try to keep it from moving on!)*

Unity may be described as the oneness, the togetherness of the composition—the blending of its various components into one unit which sets it apart and stamps it as different from any other assembly of the same component parts. It is the soul and life of any composition. It is that basic quality which its creator has breathed into it to make it different from any other. It may achieve greatness, as in a Taj Mahal or a Coliseum in architecture, or paintings such as Millet's The Gleaners, Winslow Homer's Gulf Stream, or Van Gogh's Woman of Arles; or it may be as uninspired as the average commercial Christmas card. In any event it is itself—a unit different from any other.

SCALE

Focal center out of scale

Scale correct and center of interest in proportion

Scale. Unity in the composition cannot be fully achieved unless its several component parts bear to each other an appropriate relationship in *size*. When you begin making flower arrangements, just keep in mind the nursery story of The Three Bears, each of whom had a special bed into which he fitted comfortably. Or glance about your room again, and if it is of moderate size, try to visualize how it would look with a concert grand piano jammed into one corner. You would need no authority on interior decoration to tell you that something was decidedly wrong with the décor.

In like manner, you would know instinctively that sunflowers in a small vase would not achieve a pleasing union, nor would rhododendrons and coralbells placed side by side. One or the other, very evidently, would be out of scale with the rest of the design.

A keen sense of size relationship is an asset of the greatest value to the flower arranger, perhaps second only to an accurate sense of color.

Roughly speaking, any single flower or leaf more than one third the size of the container will be out of scale. As for small flowers, these may often be used with large forms if the small ones are grouped together to form a unit similar to a compound blossom of many florets, such as phlox or azaleas.

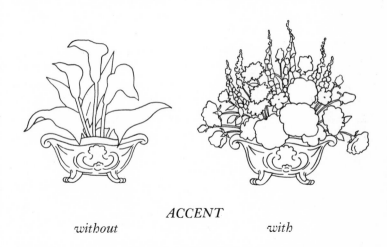

ACCENT

without   *with*

Accent. A composition may possess both unity and scale and still be completely uninteresting. The first step toward making it a better composition—a better "arrangement" where flowers are the medium employed by the artist—is to give it a center of interest by means of the use of accent, a visual focal point so strong that it dominates all the rest of the design. A glance at the arrangements on pages 81 and 84 will make evident the center of interest that each possesses.

There are several methods of attaining accent. It may be accomplished by utilizing size, color, form, contrast, or repetition in such a way as to draw attention to the focal point and to other areas of the design where less dominant accents are required. (Accent as used here applies to the composition as a whole. Other uses of accent, and methods of attaining it, are discussed in the following chapter.)

[*Suggested Exercises.* At this point we would urge the reader to do some experimenting with an assortment of flowers and foliage and a few different containers. Not many combinations need be tried before the principles enumerated above become self-evident.]

THE THREE SECONDARY PRINCIPLES

The beginner, having done some exercises as outlined above and having put together arrangements which seem to comply with the three basic principles we have been discussing, is likely to find that her efforts are less pleasing than most of the examples of good flower arrangement reproduced in these pages. The thrill which the net result of her first attempt sends along the arranger's spinal cord is not one of very high voltage.

What, then, can be done to improve her arrangements?

The first step is to study arrangements that do possess that extra something we are looking for—that quality which sets them apart from the run of the mill. Can we discover what it is?

Inspect at random any of the arrangements reproduced in this volume which especially appeal to you and, if you carefully analyze them, you will find that in each case three additional principles of design have been followed. These are:

Balance
Harmony
Rhythm

As with the principles of unity, scale, and accent, already discussed, these three apply to compositions in all forms of art.

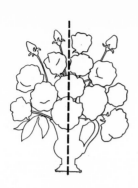
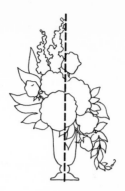

BALANCE

Symmetrical   Asymmetrical

Balance is exactly what the word implies. Any good arrangement, no matter how delicate and ethereal it may appear to be, must sit firmly on its base. At least it must *appear* to do so, for flower arrangement is a visual art, and in any visual art the eyes may readily play tricks on us. The location of a vase on the base on which it is placed may, in one position, *look* much more securely balanced than it does when placed in another position. Dark-colored flowers located at the bottom of an arrangement may appear to give it greater stability, although in reality they alter its actual balance not one iota. In any event the arrangement must seem to the observer in no danger of tipping over, in other words, to possess balance.

Balance may be either *symmetrical*, as in the arrangement on page 88 or *asymmetrical*, as in the one on page 80. It makes little difference which form it takes except that, as a general rule, an arrangement with asymmetrical balance is likely to be much more interesting than one with symmetrical balance.

Harmony, again, as the word implies, refers to the absence of any jarring note in the relationship of the several elements that go to make up the composition. It is especially important in respect to the colors used, but also as regards forms and textures.

HARMONY

Container inappropri-   *Appropriate*
ate for lotus

There is no *rule* by which harmony may be assured. It must be dictated by the artistic taste and feeling of the arranger. The illustrations on pages 72 and 73 are excellent examples in the attainment of harmony. Size, form, and color are all important factors in the selection of materials to be used in the creation of a composition. In the case of floral compositions, the most important of all is color. This subject is discussed at length in two of the following chapters.

Rhythm is more difficult to define in printer's ink than either balance or harmony. It might be defined as *frozen motion*, like that of the moving figures in Keats' *Ode on a Grecian Urn:*

"For ever piping songs for ever new . . .
For ever panting and for ever young."

RHYTHM

Lacking   *Present*

Of the several qualities we may strive to incorporate in an arrangement, effective rhythm is by far the most difficult to attain. Many never succeed in achieving such full and free rhythm as is evident in the arrangements on pages 84 and 93, but practice will bring improvement even if not inspired perfection.

[*Suggested Exercises.* Now that you have gained some idea of the general principles of composition, give yourself a test by attempting to identify them in some of the arrangements reproduced in this book. Take a post card or an envelope and cover up the captions. Then try to analyze the arrangement you are looking at in respect to the principles of design. Study them for:

Unity	Balance
Scale	Harmony
Accent	Rhythm

After you have done this, again try actually making some arrangements of your own, *keeping these three secondary principles in mind*. You will be agreeably surprised at the improvement in the results.]

6

THE ELEMENTS OF DESIGN

So far we have gained some knowledge of the qualities which a good arrangement must possess. These, taken together, are known as the principles of design.

Now let us take a look at the materials we have to work with —the building blocks, so to speak, that we will use when starting to construct the design.

There are, first of all, the *physical,* or material elements— flowers, foliage, vases or other containers, accessories (such as figurines or other objects), and backgrounds.

In this discussion, however, we are concerned not exclusively with these but with the forms, lines, spaces, the textures and colors which result when the material elements are brought together in a composition. In visual art of all types, including flower arrangement, these are known as the elements of design. It is with these that we *start* to build a composition before

ELEMENTS OF DESIGN
Form, line, spaces, textures are combined to create a unified whole.

Mrs. Richard Nathan. First Prize

A study of this composition will show the elements of design—the forms, lines, solids, and empty spaces that have been brought together to make the pattern of the arrangement, following all the principles of design. This particular arrangement is also an interesting study in the skillful use of texture.

we can make it materialize as a physical structure—a statue for the sculptor, a painting for the painter, or an arrangement for the artist working with flowers.

If you attempt to visualize an arrangement, to construct it in imagination, or to put it down in skeleton form in black and white on paper (as many good arrangers do), you will find yourself working with these elements of design which, as yet, have no physical existence.

THE BUILDING BLOCKS OF
A COMPOSITION

To see what a composition or design is made of, let us first take one apart, try to reduce it to the several elements which, when assembled, make it what it is. This is not easily done in print, but we can at least try.

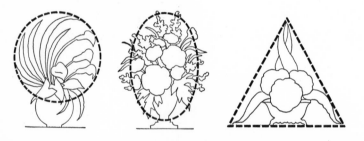

In sculpture and in other three-dimensional arts, which includes flower arrangement, the basic art forms are the sphere, the cube, the cylinder, the ellipsoid, and the pyramid.

A study of any piece of sculpture will reveal that the overall design, or pattern is based upon one of these forms. And if you look carefully at any of the arrangements reproduced in this book, you will be able to discern the basic form on which it is based. For example, the general outline of the arrangement on page 70 is that of a sphere, the one on page 93 a pyramid, the one on page 88 an ellipsoid, and so on.

In diagrams and sketches—with which we must work on the printed page—it is easier to consider these forms in *two* dimensions, *always keeping in mind, however, that in the actual construction of an arrangement its depth, or three-dimensional quality, is of supreme importance.*

When we reduce the three-dimensional forms to two dimensions, the sphere gives us a circle; the cube, a square; the ellipsoid, an ellipse; and so on.

When we use only a part of any of these two-dimensional figures, we get *line*-forms such as the semicircle, crescent, or other curve; the L, the V, the horizontal —, or the vertical | .

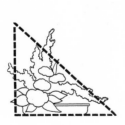

This assortment of shapes and lines are referred to as the basic forms—the elements—of design.

The moment you attempt to construct a composition of any kind, no matter how simple or how complicated, *you begin, consciously or unconsciously, to employ these.*

Mrs. John Potter

In this composition, both the principles of design (unity, scale, accent, balance, harmony, and rhythm) and the elements of design (lines, forms, open spaces, color, and texture) are well illustrated. Study it to see how effectively each has been employed.

Mrs. Howard S. Perry. Tricolor. First Prize

TEXTURE: *Here is a superb example of the employment of texture as a factor in creating a composition. Fine as this prize winner is, it would have been much less effective had not the artist stressed this quality.*

When you do become conscious of them, however, you will be able more readily to achieve the effects you seek: to create arrangements of good design. That is why we have taken pains to attempt to describe and explain these elements, even though to the reader we may have seemed to digress from our general topic.

THE ELEMENTS OF DESIGN

Now that we have some idea of what these building blocks, or elements are, we can give them names and study their particular uses in constructing compositions.

These elements are known as:

| Form | Space |
| Line | Texture |

Form. As applied to the composition as a whole, this term has reference to the over-all shape of the arrangement, or (in two dimensions) to the pattern it makes as a silhouette against its background. Thus we refer to an arrangement, in terms of form, as being spherical, pyramidal, cylindrical; or (in two-dimensional terms) circular, triangular, or vertical.

Form also applies to the *parts* that are used in constructing the composition. A triangular or a crescent-shaped flower arrangement, for instance, would be made up of circular and other typical flower and foliage forms (see illustration, page 92).

Line, in a composition, is contrasted to form in that it is an element which leads the eye of the observer along a definite path from one point to the next in an uninterrupted sequence. This line may be continuous (see page 36) or interrupted (see page 52). But it must be so self-evident that the observer's gaze will follow along it with no conscious effort on his part. In a flower arrangement, a curving stem or a sequence of blooms—related by size, form, or color—can create such a line. (A "line arrangement" is one in which these lines, or one of them, are sufficiently strong to dominate the whole composition. See page 157.)

Space may be defined, in a negative way, as an absence of form. As used in these discussions it refers to the voids, or blanks, between the forms and lines employed in the design of the arrangement. It should be noted that these "empty" areas *may be just as effective as are the materials used in determining the over-all design* (see illustration, page 81).

Texture. Dictionary definitions of texture are: "In general: the manner of structure; in artistic composition, the structure or structural quality resulting from the artist's blending of elements." The definition in the National Council of Federated Garden Clubs' *Book of Flower Shows* is: "The tissue structure or surface quality of the plant material . . . background and container."

We may speak of texture as being smooth or rough, shiny or dull, coarse or fine. As an element in composition it is especially important because it is often a decisive factor in determining what materials harmonize with each other and what do not. Harmony in texture can lend added emphasis to harmony in forms and colors. Similarly, textures that differ from each other may be used to accent contrast (see illustrations, pages 69 and 108).

The skillful employment of the use of texture may add greatly to the originality, or distinction which an arrangement possesses, and is frequently the deciding factor in whether or not it succeeds in winning an award. Texture is especially important where the colors used verge toward low or neutral values, as in many monochromatic harmonies.

Particularly should care be taken to provide texture harmony between backgrounds, accessories, containers, and the plant material used in an arrangement. Any discord here will show up more noticeably than within the arrangement itself. Many

PATTERN—the silhouette an arrangement makes against its background.

a coveted flower-show ribbon has been lost for want of greater discernment on this point. Just the right harmony or contrast in textures makes the difference.

Pattern, though sometimes spoken of as an element of design, is really not an element but rather the end result of the combination of the elements of form, line, and space. We may think of the *pattern* as the two-dimensional silhouette of a floral design, which it makes against its background.

Color. In flower arrangement, as in painting, there is another all-important element involved—that of color. It need not concern us at the moment as it is discussed in full in later chapters.

[*Suggested Exercises.* To anyone who has never had occasion to study art, even in an elementary way, the subject quite naturally is at first confusing. A careful rereading of the foregoing pages, *with a study of each of the illustrations referred to,* will help make it clearer.]

If the reader will now make a series of cutouts from catalogues and home magazines of flowers, foliage, and containers (preferably in color), she can then put them together into a two-dimensional design. Using the cutouts and the spaces between them as the elements of her design, she can give the montage an over-all design based on one of the basic forms (circle, semicircle, triangle, and so on). In it should be incorporated all of the basic principles of design (see pages 85–95), as well as the elements.

This may seem like child's play (you may not want to let your husband catch you at it), but it will be helpful. From such a montage you should be able to construct a real arrangement, just as from a rough sketch, except that this, being in color, is much better than a sketch.

If you lack the time to make cutouts or if, having made them, you want additional help, a few rough sketches of proposed arrangements will help clarify in your mind the elements and principles of design and how they should be used to create a floral composition.

7

THE PRINCIPLES OF DESIGN

In a preceding chapter devoted to the definition of flower arrangement, we spoke briefly of the general principles of design which are involved. Let us now return to them for a somewhat more detailed examination.

In the previous discussion we designated the three basic principles as *Unity*, *Scale*, and *Accent*, adding as supplementary to these, *Balance*, *Harmony*, and *Rhythm*.

Our problem now is how to make sure that we follow all of them when we attempt to design and construct a composition.

UNITY

Unity we defined as the *oneness* of the composition as a whole, its quality of being so designed and constructed that all its component parts blend in such a way as to present to the observer's eye a single picture.

As in painting, so in flower arrangement there are two general *types* of design. In one the object is merely to create something that is pleasing to the eye, that satisfies the sense of beauty; in the other the artist endeavors to express (either directly or through the more subtle association of ideas) a theme, or the interpretation of a certain emotion or idea. The former type may be said to be "decorative," the latter "expressive." Of course an expressive design also should be beautiful, but the designer should have one purpose or the other uppermost in mind when she begins to create.

Good examples of *decorative* design are to be found in the arrangements shown on pages 252 and 253, and examples of *expressive* design on pages 309 and 315.

Until comparatively recently, almost all Occidental flower arrangement was purely decorative in motif. The many "period" styles, though they differed in the plant material and in the type of containers used, were alike in that they did not attempt to convey any idea. Oriental arrangements, on the other hand, have always been designed to carry a message. Each flower and leaf, and the way in which each is placed, is a symbol which, according to long-established tradition, has a definite meaning. Good examples of both Oriental and Occidental flower art, however, conform to the principle of unity: the subservience of all the parts to one central concept—the completed composition.

UNITY is lacking in left-hand sketch because of haphazard placement of material. On right, unity is achieved.

As arrangements became an important factor in flower shows, the Oriental type, particularly the Japanese, aroused public interest and admiration. The result was a hybrid type, which has developed into our contemporary line-mass arrangement. This lacked the rigid rules and the symbolism of the Japanese, but it did much to emphasize the importance of observing the principles of design, and especially that of unity.

Mrs. Olin B. Tracy. First Prize

UNITY: In this composition (in a class calling for Caribbean Market) a large number of materials, differing widely in form and color, have been used. They have, however, been put together in such a way that the result is an integral unit in which all the parts contribute to the whole.

SCALE

Scale is the *size relationship* of the various component parts which, properly combined, make up the design. Without correct scale, complete unity cannot be achieved.

Scale applies to *all* of the component parts. In a flower arrangement these include the flowers themselves, the foliage,

Mrs. Arthur C. Kemble. Tricolor. First Prize

SCALE: *Here we have a composition in which a fine sense of scale—the size relationship of the component parts to one another—plays an important part. Despite the simplicity of the design, the effect is rich and full.*

the container, the accessories, if there are any, and the size of the arrangement in relation to its surroundings.

Even one who had never heard of such a thing as the principles of design would not use sunflowers with two or three black-eyed Susans, nor show-size dahlias in a frail bud vase, nor place a miniature (three-inches over-all) arrangement in a niche measuring eighteen by thirty inches. We all possess a sort of intuitive sense of the fitness of things concerning scale. Even

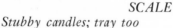
SCALE

Stubby candles; tray too small   *Scale correct*

a group of children would find something incongruous and amusing in a two-hundred-pound woman walking down the street with her head topped by a chic little pillbox of a hat the size of a tomato can.

These, of course, are extreme examples; but as you become interested in the art of flower arrangement, you will find yourself, almost without being conscious of the effort, looking for, and identifying as incorrect, much less conspicuous violations of the general principle of scale.

Another important phase of the use of scale in constructing floral compositions is correct visual *proportion* between the container and the plant material.

In general, the floral design itself looks most comfortable and happy if it is about once and a half the height of a tall container, or the width of a shallow one. Where very light, airy material is used in line designs (bittersweet or other frail vines, feathery grasses and the like), the height of the plant material may be increased to two to three times that of the container.

Examples of compositions that are in excellent scale may be found on pages 81 and 72.

ACCENT (*Focal Point or Center of Interest*)

So far, we have a composition that possesses unity and scale. And still it may be absolutely without interest, completely lacking in anything that gives it character, that invites even a second glance. What is wrong?

ACCENT

Strong accent lacking · Head creates emphatic center of interest

Study the sketches on this page and the arrangements on pages 81 and 84, and you will see. In one of the two sketches, while there is unity in the design and all the materials employed are in scale, there is no part of the arrangement that first catches and then holds the eye of the observer. Unless the eye is so caught and held, there can be nothing to engage his interest. The arrangement, because of its form and color, may be pretty to look at, but after a glance, the observer's unconscious but inevitable reaction is: "So what?"

The part of the composition (if it be a good one) which does catch the eye and holds the interest is known as the center of interest, or focal point. It is attained by *accenting* this particular section of the general design in such a way that the eye is automatically led to it, and again led back to it, no matter where the gaze may wander, just as surely as the magnetic needle of a compass swings back to *N*.

How, in a flower arrangement, is it possible to create this visual magnetic pole, this compelling center of interest?

Mrs. Herbert Blumberg

ACCENT: The creation of a center of interest may be achieved in many ways. The most usual method is to have lines or rhythmic curves, both of which have been employed here, leading to a central point. Size, color, and sharp contrast are other methods.

There are several characteristics of plant materials, and methods of combining these materials, that can be employed to achieve the desired end. They may be used separately or in combination. They are: *Form, Mass, Line, Repetition, Contrast, Gradation,* and *Color.*

FORM. The *shape* of the flower or flowers and/or foliage to be placed at the focal point. If this differs decidedly from that of the other materials used, it at once establishes a strong visual center of interest. (See diagram, page 63, and photograph, page 69.)

MASS. In the sense in which the word is used here, it implies the relative mass, or weight of the material at the desired focal point *in proportion* to that in the rest of the composition. (See diagram, page 62, and photograph, page 52.)

LINE. A branch, a stem, or a series of flowers and/or buds or leaves so placed as to lead the eye to the focal point. Usually several lines converge at this point; or a single line such as a crescent or Hogarthian curve may be employed to accomplish the same result.

If there are too many lines, or if they are of the same length or the same (visual) weight, they tend to counteract each other's effect and to result in either confusion or monotony.

A "visual" line, instead of a material one, may be used—a linear pattern formed by a series of blooms or other forms which, like steppingstones across a brook, constitute a path for the eye to follow even though they are not directly connected.

REPETITION. The repeated use of a form, a texture, or a color is still another method of building up a center of interest. In fact repetition must be used carefully in this connection, or it may become a *dis*integrating instead of an integrating factor. We recall one very carefully made show arrangement which might have captured a prize had not its creator overdone things by building up a base for it composed of three wooden blocks, each painted in one of the three colors emphasized in the arrangement itself. Needless to say, her three colored blocks did not win a tricolor ribbon.

You know what the effect is when you encounter, in prose or poetry, an author's too assiduous application of apt alliteration's artful aid, as in that couplet from Poe's *Ulalume:*

> "Come up through the lair of the Lion,
> With love in her luminous eyes."

There are only four *l*s here, but there seem to be more because all are equally accented and hit the ear like the blows of a trip hammer. Compare the effect with Tennyson's:

> "The moan of doves in immemorial elms,
> And murmuring of innumerable bees."

Here the seven *m* sounds are so skillfully blended that the reader gets the effect intended without being made conscious of the tools the artist is using to create it. Repetition should be *ob*servable, but not *ob*noxiously *ob*vious. For examples of the skillful use of repetition see illustrations on pages 73 and 295.

REPETITION AND GRADATION
Oval forms of lemons, grapes, and foliage create repetition, while their varying sizes exemplify gradation.

GRADATION, in flower arrangement as in other fields of art, means a *gradual* change in size, color, or form. It is important in connection with the center of interest because it is another means of leading the eye to the focal point of the arrangement, as, for instance, when tints or tones of a certain hue are employed in flowers farthest from the center, with gradually increasing values of the same hue being used as the center is approached. A good example of the effective use of gradation is shown on page 69.

CONTRAST AND TEXTURE
Sharp contrast in the forms and textures of lilies and monstera leaves dramatize this design.

CONTRAST. The easiest way to establish a focal point is by employing a sharp contrast with the surrounding areas, thus making a "bull's eye" that immediately fixes the observer's attention. Unless such a focal point is sufficiently related to the other materials used, however, it will defeat its own purpose by violating the very first principle of design—that of *unity*. Sharp contrasts are effective, but dangerous. The arrangement on page 84 illustrates skillful use of contrast.

COLOR. Of all the available means of establishing a dominating center of interest in an arrangement, the most effective is color. Color multiplies the visual impact of form, size, and

Mrs. John R. Bear

BALANCE: *An arrangement is in balance when the weight on each side of a vertical line through its center is approximately the same. When the pattern and the materials on both sides are identical or very similar, we have symmetrical balance, as in the arrangement above;*

when they differ, we have asymmetrical balance, as in the arrangement at the right. Accessories also play an illusive part in attaining balance, as may be seen by placing the finger tip over the bird, which appears *to lend support to the material above it, although of course it does not.*

Mrs. Rose Booth and Mrs. Bernard Farley

line. We have left it until the last in this discussion because, as yet, we have not attempted to explain what color *is* nor to describe its functions. This follows in later chapters.

BALANCE

Balance is achieved in a flower arrangement when there is an apparent effect of stability. The word "apparent" is employed because here it is the visual or psychological weight, rather than the actual physical weight, which counts. Some hues, such as red or green, seem heavier than yellow or orange; hues at full chroma seem heavier than tints, lighter than shades; white, lighter than black; with gray midway between.

BALANCE

Symmetrical—material and arrangement on each side of center identical

Asymmetrical — sides unalike but of similar visual weight.

Balance in flower arrangement is achieved when the relationship of all the component parts gives no suggestion of tipping either to the right or to the left, even if there is no actual danger of tipping over.

To accomplish this, the material used in the arrangement must be so distributed that there appears to be the same amount of weight on each side of the *central axis*—an imaginary or visual perpendicular line running up through the center of the floral design. Balance is of two types.

Symmetrical balance is attained when the elements on one side of the central axis form exactly the same pattern as those on the other. (See illustration, page 88.)

Asymmetrical balance is attained when the materials, or elements are so arranged—no matter how differently—that the total visual weight on one side equals that on the other. (See illustration, page 88.) In general, asymmetrical arrangements afford much more opportunity for the use of originality and dramatic effect than do those which follow a strictly symmetrical pattern; and for this reason they are much more likely to prove interesting.

VISUAL BALANCE
The eye tells us that the lengths of bamboo at far left destroy balance, while, as placed at the right, they firmly establish it.

To a gardener these two types of balance are not new. He will have employed both in laying out his grounds: symmetrical balance when he plants identical or matched groups of evergreens at either side of a doorway; asymmetrical when he has "balanced" one tall evergreen or a large shrub on one side of a gate or arbor by placing a group of smaller forms on the other.

In achieving either type of balance in a flower arrangement, the following facts should be kept in mind:

1. The farther away from the central axis a flower, bud, or leaf is placed, the greater will be its apparent weight.

2. The darker the color of the element, the greater its apparent weight. A dark red rose, for instance, actually weighs no more than a white one of the same size, but *visually* will tip the scales against it.

3. The higher up in the arrangement an element is placed, the greater its apparent weight.

HARMONY

When we speak of harmony in an arrangement, we begin to deal with intangibles, with aesthetic qualities rather than

HARMONY
The tall slim vase and small base at left are inadequate for heavy fig branches and hydrangea blooms; right, heavy burl base and sturdy jar are harmonious and establish needed weight for good balance.

with physical properties. Personal reactions differ widely on what constitutes harmony in the relationship to each other of the parts of a composition, but there are general limits. A combination of spring-flowering crocus and summer-flowering gladiolus, for instance, would usually be incongruous and therefore not harmonious either in seasonal relationship or in size.

The same would be true of a combination of orchids and zinnias. Even though in color they might be entirely congruous, they would still be most unsuited to one another.

HARMONY: That subtle "going togetherness" which is difficult to define, but the presence or absence of which always makes itself felt. Here we have unusually good harmony in the flower, fruit, and foliage forms, in the muted colors, and especially in textures.

Coarse-textured flowers and foliage placed in an elegant container of silver or glass are, as a rule, disturbing in effect even if the arrangement has perfect scale and balance and a strong center of interest.

Mrs. Frederick Lewis

RHYTHM: Perhaps more than any other one factor, rhythm can lend distinction to an arrangement. There are many ways of producing an effect of rhythmic motion, but if they become over-obvious they begin to defeat their own purpose. In this composition the theme established by the unusually expressive figurine is well carried along by the plant material.

In a word, you know when you look at a building or a painting or listen to a musical composition whether it is "harmonious" or whether somewhere there seems to be a discordant, jarring note—a lack of harmony—even if you can't be certain just what it is. The same holds true for a flower arrangement.

When it comes to color, we can be somewhat more certain where harmony ends and disharmony begins. (See the discussion of color in Chapter 9.) Even here, of course, the experts disagree, sometimes violently. But any distinct disharmony is obvious to almost any observer, even if he cannot tell exactly what is wrong. The arrangements on pages 92 and 41 are particularly good examples of harmony, the first in *design*, the second in *color*.

RHYTHM

And now we come to perhaps the most intangible and illusive of all the principles of design—that of *rhythm*.

In flower arrangement it may be described as what we have already termed "frozen motion." It is the employment of line

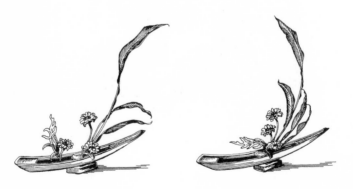

RHYTHM

Material placed at di-   *Design here suggests*
vergent angles   *rhythmic motion*

or accent in such a way that the observer gets the *effect* of motion, even though the materials he is looking at are static.

How is this accomplished?

It is difficult to put into words, but a study of such arrangements as those shown on pages 93, 84, and 156 will make clear what is meant by rhythm and indicate the means by which it is accomplished. Any curved line which not only leads to the center of interest but *sweeps on through it* to the outer edges of the composition helps create the sense of rhythm. The eye follows it to the end and then returns, again and again, just as it will follow a wave advancing toward the shore and then return to pick up another.

The single sweep of a crescent, or the double one of a Hogarthian curve, are the most effective lines in creating a sense of rhythm.

The line may be either a continuous one, as in the arrangements on pages 36 and 84, or it may be established by *repetition* (explained on page 85). Mastery of rhythm will do more than any other one skill to give your arrangements interest and distinction.

8

NOW WE COME TO COLOR

Up to this point we have been discussing the art of arranging flowers from the point of view of design, emphasizing the principles of design—form, line, scale, balance, proportion, and the like. Now we come to *color*, which, throughout our study of the subject, has been fluttering around in the background like a butterfly over a Buddleia bush. Flowers just cannot be divorced from color, so now we must take the plunge into it.

Color is the fourth dimension that brings life, zip, added dramatic quality to a good arrangement. It sometimes even conceals faults that would otherwise be evident. This is true to such an extent that even experienced judges have to be on guard against letting it sway their decisions—and this is a very serious matter, for if there is anything in the world more serious than a team of judges at a flower show, we have yet to encounter it.

There are two sound reasons why we have delayed the discussion of color until this point. First, it is easier for the beginner to get a conception, in black and white, of the principles of composition and design before the complications which color brings in are added. Second, any discussion of color, to be helpful, must be based upon some knowledge of what color *is*.

To the beginner, no phase of the art of flower arrangement seems so complicated as that of the use of color. Even the terms employed by writers and lecturers in discussing color are by no means standardized or uniform. The result is that many a dissertation on the subject merely leaves the novice in confusion worse confounded. Our purpose here is to go into the subject of color—at least the A,B,C of a working knowledge of it—in terms that may readily be understood.

THE THEORY OF COLOR

To imply that any adequate presentation of the world of color could be given in a single chapter of a book would indeed be presumptuous. What we do hope to be able to do is put the reader on a speaking acquaintance with it.

First of all it must be recognized that color, like sound, is not a physical entity but merely a sensation, a sensation that is a result of stimuli from outside, transmitted to the brain through a specialized organ of the body. This organ, in the case of sound, is the ear; with color, the eye. The various "colors" of which we speak do not have any physical identities in the sense in which we ordinarily think of them. They are the results of varying *light rays*, just as the different notes in a musical scale are the result of sound waves.

The fact that colors need have no physical embodiment is easily demonstrated. All you need are a piece of white paper and a glass prism. Hold the latter so that it catches a shaft of direct sunlight. This white shaft, passing through the prism, is spread out upon the paper as a multicolored band with red at one end and violet at the other.

Where do these colors come from?

They appear because each of the several light rays (all bound up together in the "white" sunshine) has its own angle of refraction and, as it passes through the prism, is bent according to its own particular angle. The multicolored band that results (see page 101) is known as the solar spectrum. This spectrum forms the basis for the definition of the various colors we know as red, blue, yellow, and so on. (These are the colors which the human eye can perceive. Beyond them are the invisible light rays—ultraviolet at one end and infrared at the other.)

Now let's take our spectrum and bend it around into a circle with the ends touching—like a serpent swallowing its own tail. This gives us the "color circle"—that mystic symbol which holds such a high place in the ceremonies of the high priestesses of flower arrangement. Such a circle is shown on page 101. In reality, however, the colors are not marked off into neat little sections as they are in a printed color circle; they run together, or blend so that it is impossible to say where one ends and the next begins. For purposes of discussion we cut the circle up into segments. Different authorities do this in different ways. Usually the pie is cut into six slices—YELLOW, GREEN, BLUE, VIOLET, RED, and ORANGE.

Then, in order that each member of the color family may have a piece of the pie, each of these six is again cut into three, giving us a total of eighteen. These smaller slices are designated as ORANGE-YELLOW and GREEN-YELLOW, YELLOW-GREEN and BLUE-GREEN, and so on around the circle.

We have been speaking of these divisions as different colors. More accurately they may be designated as different "hues."

In the Rockwell Color Chart on page 101 we show at the top a band representing the solar spectrum from violet-red to red-violet. Bending this into a ring, we have produced the color circle in the center. The pure, unadulterated *hues* appear in the second band of the circle, dulled on the inner band to *shades* by adding black and paled to *tints* on the outer band by adding white. (See also pages 103–5.) Below the wheel is a strip of seven squares, a pure red *hue* at the center. To the left are three squares to which white has been added to make *tints* until, at the exteme left, no red hue remains. Right of center appear three squares dulled to *shades* by adding black until, at the exteme right, no trace of red remains. (See also pages 104 and 105.)

PRISMATIC AND PIGMENT COLOR

The hues which we observe when a shaft of light is passed through a prism are known as prismatic colors. These are the hues which one sees in a full rainbow or observes, to some extent, in the droplets of water from a lawn sprinkler when the sun is shining through them. There is no way of capturing these true colors; they are as un-material as the notes of a sonata played on a violin, or the wind-stirred "horns of Elfland, faintly blowing." Together they form what is known as the prismatic spectrum.

How then do we capture these colors which have no material existence? It is done simply by making use of substances which have the capacity to reflect some parts of a shaft of white light and to absorb others. These substances, which we call pigments, act as sentries, allowing some of the light rays to pass and halting others. Those which are permitted to pass (or more accurately, are reflected) strike the eye. Those which are absorbed are stopped in their tracks and so we fail to "see" them. Pigments, or surfaces to which pigments such as paints or dyes are applied, thus provide us with the colors of everyday use. Pigments which reflect *all* of the elements in a shaft of light are seen as white. Those which absorb all are seen as black.

By mixing together these pigments in varying proportions, we can provide a full range of colors as indicated by the color chart shown. While they are not exactly like the hues revealed in the prismatic or solar spectrum, they are, to all intents and purposes, reasonable facsimiles thereof.

COLOR VALUES:
SHADES, TINTS, AND TONES

So far so good. We have taken a first step toward arriving at a basis for recognizing and discussing color in terms of the individual hues which, taken together, constitute color. But at once we run into another problem, for there are hundreds of colors other than those we find in traveling around the color circle. What about them?

Let us go back for a moment to the solar or prismatic spectrum on the sheet of white paper. The paper is *white* because it is of a substance that *reflects* all of the many light rays combined in the shaft of sunlight. If we substitute a paper that

THE "VOCABULARY" OF COLOR

THE SPECTRUM

The straight band across the top of the opposite page is a reproduction of the solar *spectrum, obtained by passing a ray of sunlight through a prism. This gives a series of pure colors, or "hues," ranging from red at one end to violet at the other, with orange, yellow, green, and blue in between.*

THE COLOR CIRCLE

When the hues of the spectrum—or others approximating them—are arranged in the form of a ring, we have a color circle. (See the middle one of the three concentric rings shown opposite.) The number of pure colors, or hues, varies with different color "systems"; here there are six—red, orange, yellow, green, blue, violet. These are termed primary *hues. The divisions in between—such as violet-red, orange-red—are termed* secondary *hues.*

SHADES, TINTS, AND TONES

The addition of black, white, or gray (a combination of black and white) to any of these hues will produce a new color. Black produces a shade; *white a* tint, *and gray a* tone. *The amount of black, white, or gray determines the variations. Thus, in the band at the bottom of the opposite page, black and white added to orange-red give, respectively, progressive shades and tints of this hue.*

COLOR HARMONIES

Certain combinations of color form "harmonies." A monochromatic *harmony consists of shades, tints, and tones of the same hue; an* analogous *harmony, colors adjacent to each other on the circle (such as violet, red-violet, and blue-violet); a* complementary *harmony, colors opposite each other (orange and blue). Of the complementary harmonies several types are described in this chapter.*

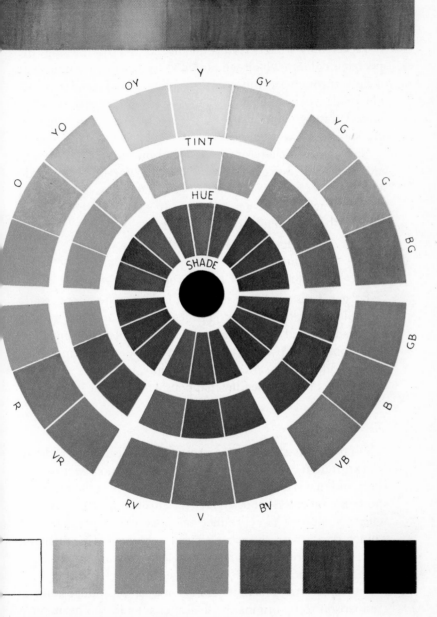

Y
OY   GY
YO   YG
O   G
                   BG
TINT
HUE
SHADE
                   GB
R   B
VR   VB
RV   BV
V

THE ROCKWELL COLOR CHART

Executed by John Brimer

absorbs all the light rays, a *black* paper, then the spectrum disappears altogether! White is a combination of all the hues in the spectrum—a fact readily demonstrated by passing the spectrum colors (which we obtained by passing a white shaft of light through a prism) on through a *second*, similar prism. The result will be that the colorful spectrum reappears as white light! White is a combination of all colors. Black (though usually spoken of as a color) is really the *absence* of all colors.

Now if we take any one of the hues on the color circle and add black to it, we get a "shade" of the same hue. If we add white, we get a "tint." If we add gray (which is a mixture of black and white), we get a "tone." In each case, however, it remains the same hue. To recapitulate:

> Adding black to a hue produces a *shade*.
> Adding white to a hue produces a *tint*.
> Adding gray to a hue produces a *tone*.

To get a visual demonstration of these differences, study carefully the color triangles on pages 104 and 105. Here a single hue (jade or red) at the apex of the triangle is changed, in three directions, by the additions of black, white, and gray, thus producing the series of shades, tints, and tones shown in the triangle. (The same thing happens with any hue so treated.)

CHROMA

So far we have made some progress in measuring, or identifying different colors. There is, however, one more fact to consider, and that is chroma, or intensity. The hues in the prismatic spectrum, or color band, are at full chroma, or intensity; but when we attempt to reproduce them by use of *pigments*, we cannot reincarnate them with exact accuracy. The pigments used, the texture of the surface to which they are applied, and the light in which they are viewed are all factors affecting what the eye perceives. The more closely we can reproduce a hue in comparison to its original prismatic character, the nearer it is to "full" chroma.

In using flowers, we deal with both reflected and translucent colors (that is, those with light shining through them). So here we have another problem when we attempt to match these hues with those represented on a color chart made with pigments.

WHITE, BLACK, AND NEUTRAL COLORS

While we speak of white and black as colors, there are no such hues in the color circle. In reality, as we have seen, white is a combination of all the prismatic hues and black the absence of all. With pigments, white is a surface which reflects all of the hues in the prismatic spectrum, and black a surface which absorbs them all.

When exact opposites, or complementary, hues in the color circle are combined, they cancel each other out and create gray. The same thing happens when gray, in sufficient amounts, is added to an individual hue: its value, or chroma is gradually diminished to the point where it can no longer be identified as belonging to any particular hue represented on the color circle. Hence black, white, and gray are known as neutral colors.

[*Suggested Exercises.* This analysis of color, and the discussions of its physical aspects, will prove helpful when we come to the part that color plays in flower arranging. We would, however, suggest that any reader who has never had occasion to work with color try a few simple experiments.

If a set of tempera colors, including the color-circle hues of yellow, orange, green, blue, red, and also black and white, are procured, it will be an easy matter for the student to construct a color chart and then, by experimental mixing, to obtain the intermediate hues shown on the color wheel on page 101 and those shown on the color triangle on page 104.]

By actually handling the colors themselves, the student will remember the facts in the preceding pages more permanently and more thoroughly than she would merely by reading the printed words. If she cares to invest in an inexpensive glass prism, she will find it a most fascinating gadget and a further aid in comprehending the complex world of color.

WHITE

COLOR

BLACK

COLOR TRIANGLE: Starting with the hue (at extreme left), black is added, in increasing amounts, in the lower line of squares, giving a series of ever-deepening shades. In the same way, white added (in the upper row of squares) gives a series of tints; and gray (across the center) a series of tones. Courtesy of Faber Birren

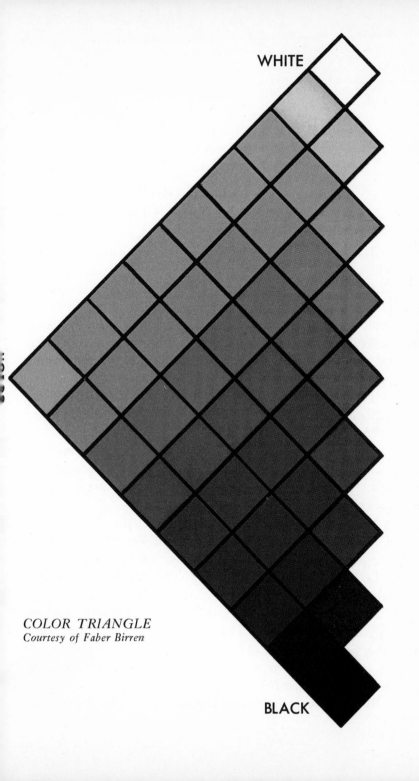

WHITE

COLOR TRIANGLE
Courtesy of Faber Birren

BLACK

9

THE USE OF COLOR IN ARRANGEMENTS

By this time the reader is probably beginning to wonder what all this discussion about color has to do with actually making flower arrangements. Do not get impatient. The successful employment of color is the very soul of modern flower arrangement. However, you cannot just use color, no matter how generously, in a hit-or-miss way, and expect to construct arrangements that will capture blue ribbons—or, for that matter, give any measure of satisfaction even to yourself.

To make certain that your arrangements will be really pleasing, you must employ colors *in proper relationship to each other*.

This relationship is twofold. First comes the relationship to each other of any colors used. Some combinations are pleasing and others are not. The former we term color *harmonies*, and the others are color discords.

Next, there is the relationship of the colors to the *design*. They must be placed in accord with the general principles of design which have already been discussed in a previous chapter.

Let us first consider the relationship of different hues to each other.

For most persons, certain combinations of color seem to "go together"—to harmonize. Other combinations "scream at each other"—are discordant. How can we tell which combinations are going to be harmonious and which are not? Are there any rules to be followed?

Rules in plenty have been laid down, but you will get far

more help from a few basic principles. As is the case with design, so with the employment of color, no set of rules can assure success. There are guiding principles, but before these are stated we need a few more definitions.

Just why some combinations are pleasing to most persons while others are displeasing, no one can say. The matter of preferences is a racial or cultural inheritance, just as is the feeling concerning harmonies or discords in music. The monotonous beat of a tom-tom may be music to a savage who would be bored to death with an étude; the untutored girl of the story goes into a dress shop and asks for something simple and quiet —"just plain red and yaller." We just have to accept the fact that among Western civilizations some combinations of color are considered to be harmonious while others are discordant.

The use of color in decorating rooms, from the point of view of their psychological effect on those who occupy them, has, during recent years, been given much attention. It is generally recognized that some colors are stimulating, exhilarating, others actually depressing. We need not explore this fascinating field far, but we can take a leaf or two from its book for practical application in the making of flower arrangements.

In general it may be said that the nearer we can get to pure hues (colors at their fullest chroma, or intensity), the more attention-compelling and stimulating they are. Most zinnias and marigolds, for instance, come in intense colors, and a bowl of them in a sunny window well illustrates this point. Most petunias and asters, on the contrary, come in tints, or shades and are much less dramatic—although they may be just as pleasing—in their impact on the observer.

Tints of pure hues have a cheerful, uplifting effect; pink roses combined with light blue delphiniums would illustrate this point. *Shades* have the opposite effect: in direct proportion as they approach black, they tend to become depressing, especially if they are not counterbalanced by contrasting lighter or brighter colors. *Tones* are quieting, soothing in their effect. Many of the monochromatic arrangements made with dried materials, such as that shown on page 252, fall into this category.

Mrs. George J. Hirsch

In this composition, employing the colors in American Indian arts and crafts, it is proved that even in a polychromatic, or multi-colored design, discriminating selection of tints, tones, and shades can produce a completely harmonious and unified whole.

A comparable difference is to be found in respect to the several *hues* themselves, regardless of their chroma, or intensity. Yellow, which we instinctively associate with sunshine, is a cheerful color. Red suggests warmth; green, coolness; blue, tranquillity; violet, a touch of the spiritual, for want of a better word.

Warm and Cool Colors. Study carefully the color circle on page 101 and try to analyze your reactions as your eyes travel from one hue to the next. Red, instinctively associated with fire, gives very definitely the effect of warmth. Green, suggesting a shady nook or a curling wave, carries with it an effect of coolness. The hues adjacent to red and green also suggest warmth and coolness, respectively, but in diminishing degrees as they approach yellow and violet.

Advancing and Receding Colors. In still another respect, the various hues differ in their psychological effect. The warmest, red, orange, and magenta, are *advancing* in character; they are aggressive and seem to come at you. All of the cool hues, from green to blue-violet, are, on the contrary, retiring, *receding*. They suggest distance, a fact that both the landscape artist and the interior decorator often take advantage of in planning a garden or a room where space is limited.

Discussion of the psychological values of colors is not just empty, theoretical jargon. These characteristics of color do have a practical, everyday application in the art of flower arranging, even in so simple a matter as making bouquets for the home.

All this discussion is not intended to imply that when you think of making a flower arrangement you will sit down and decide, first of all, just what mood you wish to throw the observer into as a result of his viewing it—and then go out and cut your flowers, or buy them, accordingly. It is, nevertheless, *usable* information that, carried in the back of your mind, will contribute to your ability to make better and more interesting arrangements. If you wish to make a particularly cheerful bouquet—as one for a sickroom—you will not use blooms in somber shades. If you desire a cool effect for a room in midsummer, you won't select an armful of salvia or blazing red gladiolus with which to accomplish your purpose.

If, however, you are making an "interpretive" composition for competition in a flower show, then you will make very *conscious* use of your knowledge of the psychological effect of colors on the observer.

COLOR HARMONIES

In color we have two general types of harmonies: those which are neighbors on the color wheel and live side by side, and those which are strangers and live across the wheel from each other. The former are called "related" and the latter "contrasted" harmonies.

In the related harmonies there are two types:

Monochromatic harmonies are made up of variations *of the same hue:* shades, tones, and tints of a single spectrum color. There may be a variation of chroma also, best effected by using flowers, foliage, and accessories of different textures. There must, however, be no straying to right or left on the color wheel (page 101). If the monochrome is to be in blue-violet, for instance, neither violet on one side nor red-violet on the other are admissible.

Analogous harmonies include colors *adjacent* to each other on the color circle, as, for instance, blue, green-blue, and violet-blue. It may be stretched to include also the next two adjacent hues, blue-green and blue-violet; but this is reaching the *verboten* line and can be done successfully only if there is careful gradation, with intermediate hues between the two extremes. The beginner will do well to stick to three adjacent hues, with their tones, tints, and shades—all of which may be employed.

Coming now to the contrasted (complementary) harmonies, we find:

Direct Complementary harmony, in which two hues directly opposite each other on the color circle are used together, and/or their tones, tints, and shades.

Near Complementary: Any hue, with *either* (but not both) of the two hues adjacent to its complement. Example: yellow, and either red-violet *or* blue-violet.

Split Complementary: A hue on one side of the color circle, combined not with its direct opposite but with one on each side of the direct opposite. Example: red, plus yellow-green and blue-green—but *not green itself.*

Double Split Complementary: In this, the complement, so to speak, is returned; for *each* of two directly opposite hues is combined with the two side-kicks of its opposite, making a free-for-all of six hues, and no holds barred!

Paired Complementary: Four hues, in two adjacent direct complements, as orange-yellow and yellow-orange, with blue-violet and blue-green—thus forming an *X* on the color wheel.

Adjacent Complement: Three hues; one, and its direct complement, plus one of the adjacent hues on either side of it. Example: green and red, plus red-orange *or* red-violet.

Analogous Complement: Any three adjacent hues, plus the direct complement of any one of them, making a total of four. Example: blue, blue-green, and blue-violet, plus orange (*or* yellow-orange *or* red-orange).

Diad: Any two hues separated by two adjacent colors. Example: orange and yellow-green; *or* orange and red-violet.

Triad: Three hues that are equidistant from each other on the color circle. Example: yellow, blue, and red; *or* red-orange, yellow-green, and blue-violet.

In all these combinations it is most important to note that while HUES *only are mentioned, there should be—in fact it is safe to say that there* MUST *be—gradations in the shades, tones, and tints of the hues employed if a pleasing result is to be achieved. Furthermore, the chroma, or intensity of the hues is a factor, as is also the* AREA *assigned to each. It is the good judgment used in the handling of these variables that determines the measure of the artist's skill.*

A careful study of the arrangements on pages 112 and 113 will emphasize the point.

Mrs. George Goldson   *Mrs. George Goldson. Tricolor; First Prize*

(Left) MONOCHROMATIC HARMONY: One hue, with its tones, tints, and shades.
(Right) ANALOGOUS HARMONY: Colors adjacent to each other on the color circle, as blue, blue-green, and blue-violet; or violet, blue-violet, and red-violet.

So much, then, for the relationships of colors to each other, and the desirability of fostering friendships among them and avoiding discordant quarrels. But before we proceed to our ultimate goal of fitting colors successfully into the design, there is one further color quality to be considered.

COLOR IN RELATION TO PLANNING
THE ARRANGEMENT

To create any design worthy of the name, the designer must have in mind some idea of the *effect* that is being sought. Per-

Mrs. Harry Chooljian   *Mrs. Charles A. Hollis*

(Left) COMPLEMENTARY HARMONY: Two hues directly opposite each other on the color circle, such as red and green or their tones, tints, or shades.

(Right) TRIAD: Three colors equidistant from each other on the color circle, as yellow, blue, and red; or red-orange, yellow-green, and blue-violet.

haps this objective is not quite so definite as it is in the case of a composer, for instance, who knows very definitely whether he wishes to produce a gay and lively piece that will set the listeners' feet to dancing, a waltz that will carry them away in evenly swaying, dreamy gyrations, or a funeral dirge that would suggest the slow, measured tread. The arranger, however, has—or should have—an idea of the emotional reaction the proposed composition will create.

This is where the psychology of color, as the experts like to call it, enters the picture. In reality it is just the common sense of color.

Color harmonies, which we have just discussed, also have strong psychological effects, often more compelling than those of the individual colors themselves. Note the arrangements on pages 108 and 285.

With these necessary definitions of color terms and this rather meager discussion of the psychological effects of color behind us, we now turn to the more practical matter of how to *use* color in constructing an arrangement.

In our previous discussion of design (in Chapter 7) we found that the principles to be followed were the primary ones of *Unity, Scale, Accent*, plus the secondary ones of *Balance, Harmony*, and *Rhythm*. Now these old friends bob up again in a new guise. They serve as the guards standing at the gate to decide just what details of construction shall be allowed to pass and which shall not.

Artistic sense and good taste say that in the pattern of colors we employ there must be a distinctive design which forms a unit; that the areas of color used must follow a scale relationship to each other; that there must be a center of interest to which the eye is drawn by the color pattern; that the areas of color must constitute visual balance, either symmetrical or asymmetrical; that the colors must harmonize with each other; and that they shall adjoin each other in such a way that the beholder's eye, following them, shall consciously or unconsciously catch a distinct sense of rhythm.

Thus it becomes evident that when we apply color to the composition (as inevitably we must in arranging flowers), we are in fact making a combination of *two* designs—one of *forms*, the other of *colors*. We have, in effect, a design within a design, or superimposed one upon the other.

In discussing them, it is important to keep these two types of design separated, although in the arrangement itself they are, of course, blended into a unified whole. The sketch on page 79 and the illustration on page 136 illustrate what we mean by a "design within a design." In the former, all hues are of equal value, and the result gives a monotonous, undramatic effect. In the latter, the design of *forms* is almost exactly the same, but the *colors* are distributed to emphasize the design which they themselves form.

The result is that *both* the form-design and the color-design conform to the requirements of good composition.

Unity in the use of color is attained when the hues employed (with their various tones, tints, shades, and chroma intensities) conform to the accepted standards of color harmonies already discussed (page 110). The arrangement on page 80 has excellent color unity, that on page 212 is less perfect in this respect.

Scale. When we come to scale in the color design, we have a somewhat different problem than is the case when we are dealing with forms. The visual impact of some hues is much greater than that of others, and this must be taken into account. An area of red at full chroma has many times the force of the same area of a light tint, or a dark shade, of red. The dark shade of red, in turn, is more forceful than the tint. Orange, in any value, has more impact than violet at the same intensity. For this reason, all of the "advancing" hues—red, orange, and yellow—*seem* to occupy more space than similar areas of green, blue, or violet, just as a bed of Red Emperor tulips or scarlet sage seem, when seen from a little distance, to loom larger in the landscape than a similar area planted with vinca minor or heliotrope.

ACCENT

In considering accent as applied to form design, we spoke of several distinct methods of achieving it: form; mass, with its concomitant proportion; line; color; repetition; contrast; and gradation.

In applying color, we have the same factors, but *contrast* and *repetition* become relatively much more important than they were in the former case.

To realize this we have but to observe specimens of individual flowers. The tiniest spot of contrasting color at the heart creates a center of interest which the eye cannot help focusing upon. The bit of gold in the stamens of a blue tradescantia or a deep red single rose, the cluster of dark anthers trembling at the center of a bright tulip are examples of the bull's-eye effect of a strongly contrasting hue, no matter how small in area it may be. They emphasize the power of contrast, where color is involved, in establishing a focal point. A single bloom of a sharply contrasting hue can determine the center of interest in a flower arrangement.

In employing color for this purpose, however, there are two factors that should be given very careful consideration. The first is that the *color* focal point and the *design* focal point shall coincide; otherwise, there will be two conflicting centers of interest, competing with each other and thus destroying unity in the design.

The second is that the color focal point shall not create too violent a contrast, resulting in a color discord instead of a complementary color harmony.

The above comments apply also to the use of repetition. A series of unrelated color areas in the arrangement that stand out sharply will result in a polka-dot effect that distracts the eye and interferes with the center of interest, instead of leading the eye to it. A good example of the effective use of repetition may be seen in the arrangement on page 156.

Gradation. The gradation of colors, if skillfully handled, is one of the most potent factors in the creation of arrangements that have artistic distinction and mark the really competent arranger as compared to the amateur. Here the "eye for color" —if one is so fortunate as to possess it—becomes the dictator of just which flowers are to be used together.

As a general rule, it is best to keep those of strongest color (nearest to full chroma) near the center and work out from this with hues of gradually decreasing intensity (tints, tones, or shades) toward the edges. The use of foliage that verges toward gray, such as that of artemisia, rex begonia, or mullein, will be helpful here, as it has a double effect: its own tone and a slight graying down of the colors adjacent to it.

The word of caution here is to avoid building up a series of concentric circles, resulting in a target effect. Let your color gradations follow the form of the design—a crescent, a Hogarthian curve leading to the focal point, or a pyramid. The color gradations will then subtly emphasize the over-all design. (Study the arrangements on pages 36 and 73.)

Mass and proportion, form and line. The remarks on pages 84 to 86 concerning these principles, subsidiaries to the more important principle of Accent, apply also to the use of color. We need not repeat them here.

BALANCE, HARMONY, AND RHYTHM IN COLOR

When we come to the consideration of balance in connection with color, we are dealing with intangibles. *Color*, being merely a result of light rays striking the optic nerve, does not have any actual weight. But different hues *seem* to vary in weight, and that is what counts as we look at any composition in which color plays a part.

The warm, or advancing colors—red, yellow, and orange—appear to weigh more than the cool, or receding colors—violet, blue, and green. Moreover, darkening values of any hue, approaching black, appear to weigh more than tints, approaching white. Shades, approaching gray or "middle value," are between the two in apparent weight. A glance at the color triangle on page 105 will make this fact evident; and a study of the arrangements on pages 161 and 253 will further demonstrate it.

It follows that the more nearly these "heavy" colors are kept to the center of the arrangement and the lower down toward the base, the more securely balanced the composition will *appear* to be.

Harmony. The discussion of color harmonies earlier in this chapter leaves little more to be said on this point, except that we have not yet considered the importance of surroundings —in the home, the location of the arrangement; in a flower show, the niche—as affecting the arrangement as a whole. The color of the background alone can do much to help make or destroy the effect of the composition. (See illustrations, pages 161 and 232.)

The same is also true of containers and accessories, material elements in the composition as a whole. We have seen many examples, in flower shows, where a container, because of its color, simply split the over-all design in two. This may happen even when the color of the container forms, in theory, a complementary harmony with the flower colors used, but is not carefully tied in to the design as a whole.

Rhythm. Here color should follow the lines which lead the eye to the focal point, the chroma, and/or the intensity of the hues employed being increased as the focal point is approached. (See illustration on page 93.) The attainment of successful rhythm in the use of color is one of the most difficult of all the principles of design to carry out. But the more conscious the arranger becomes of its importance, the better her arrangements are likely to be.

Part Three

TYPES OF ARRANGEMENTS

10

ORIENTAL FLOWER ART

CHINESE

From ancient Chinese culture, with its many art forms and media of expression, flower and plant motifs are preserved in paintings, prints, and scrolls. These include cut blossoms of peonies, chrysanthemums, and other flowers, branches of flowering fruits and other living plant material informally arranged in handsome vases. This phase of Chinese art reached its height during the eleventh and twelfth centuries under the Sung Dynasty, but floral designs abound also in the Ming and Ch'ing Dynasties, as discussed in Chapter 2. One of the greatest flower artists of the Ch'ing period in the seventeenth century, Ting Liang-hsien, using colored wood-block prints as his medium, portrayed exquisite vases holding peonies, camellias, fruit blossoms, and other plant material flanked by boxes, scrolls, incense burners, and similar art objects.

Chinese gardens, conceived and executed with all the vision and artistry of fine paintings, lie in the realm of landscape architecture rather than of flower arrangement, yet there is a close relationship between the two since both are based on the principles of design and both are created with plant material and accessory objects—works of art appealing to the eye because of their balanced beauty, and to the spirit through symbolism.

In China the use of cut flowers as temple offerings and in the home, though less stylized than in Japan, has always been a recognized art form, a fact proved by the paintings and prints extant from the most ancient times.

Little consideration was given to Chinese flower art by Western arrangers until World War II made Japanese flower arrangement temporarily unpopular. Students were aware of the fact that the Japanese art stemmed from the Chinese, just as do other phases of Japanese culture. It was natural, therefore,

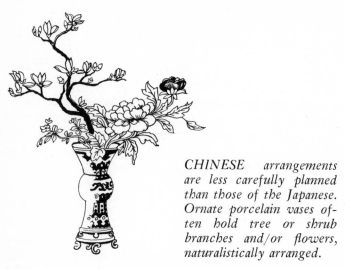

CHINESE arrangements are less carefully planned than those of the Japanese. Ornate porcelain vases often hold tree or shrub branches and/or flowers, naturalistically arranged.

that during this period Western floral artists should delve into the history and development of this art form in China. Though it can show no such concentration of effort as that of Japan, we can and do still acknowledge China as the source or fountainhead of Oriental flower art, the dominant characteristic of which is unstudied natural beauty, as opposed to the set traditions and hidebound rules of classical Japanese arrangement.

In general, the Chinese way with flowers includes the use in each composition of the strong, erect, highly colored and dominant male element, *yang;* and the smaller, finer, delicately tinted and formed horizontal or vinelike female element, *ying.* The nice combination of these two make for perfection in Chinese arrangement, the emphasis being on naturalism, not stylized design. As a rule, not more than two species are placed in one vase, for, unlike Western taste, to Chinese eyes a number of different varieties of flowers and foliage crowded together in one vase is not to be admired, no matter how well the composition may be designed.

Toward the close of the sixteenth century, Chang Ch'ien-tê wrote a treatise on "Vase Flowers" which contained the following advice:

"If a single branch is used, select one that is of curious and aged appearance, one which is gnarled and crooked. When two different kinds of flowers are used, they should be of different heights and, when placed together, look as if they were grown naturally from a single stalk. . . .

"Only one or two kinds of flowers should be arranged in a vase. If too many different kinds are used together, they are unappealing."

CONTAINERS

No other country has produced more distinguished vases than those of old China, many of which are among the most cherished art objects in the world. Containers include beautiful bronze, pewter, porcelain, and pottery vases, jars, low dishes, cups, and bottles; some are intricately decorated, others in chaste neutral glazes ideal for displaying flowers. Baskets of many shapes are also traditional.

Bases. As in Japanese flower art, bases are customarily used in China, except under baskets. Vases and dishes are placed on stands or taborets of carved teakwood or on solid bases of porcelain, pottery, or wood.

PLANT MATERIAL

Seasonal plant material is always used in China, and each month of the year has its special flowers dedicated to arrangement.

From early times these blossoms, branches, leaves, and fruits have symbolized for the Chinese people the particular season in which each blooms or bears. Some, like the tree peony, the lotus, and the Japanese apricot, are always dominant in any arrangement in which they are placed, while others occupy subordinate positions. Many have symbolic meanings as well as seasonal significance.

The following chart is designed to give a rudimentary idea of how the Chinese use cut flowers to express seasonal greetings, friendly messages, sympathy, and other emotions.

WINTER FLOWERS

DOMINANT	*Symbolic Meanings*
Camellia japonica	
*Japanese apricot	Felicity, perseverance, and purity
Juniper	The winter solstice
Pine	Wisdom, longevity, and nobility
SUBORDINATE	
Bamboo	Longevity, constancy, humility, and fidelity
Camellia Sasanqua	
Jasmine nudiflora	
Nandina	
Narcissus (Chinese sacred-lily)	Prosperity, good fortune, and purity

EARLY SPRING

DOMINANT	
Azalea	
Cymbidium virescens	Sincere friendship, nobility
Daphne odora	
Japanese plum (with peach blossoms)	Brotherhood and friendship
Magnolia	
Peach blossoms	Youth, charm
SUBORDINATE	
Camellia reticulata	
Crab-apple	
Willow	Feminine grace, mercy
Wisteria	

*indicates the most important and distinguished flower of each season.

LATE SPRING

DOMINANT
Apricot
*Tree peony   Wealth, aristocracy
Camellia japonica

SUBORDINATE
Daphne Genkwa
Lilac

EARLY SUMMER

DOMINANT
Cymbidium ensifolium
*Lotus   Purity, nobility
Herbaceous peony   Wealth, rank

SUBORDINATE
Day-lily   Purity
Oleander
Rose
Silk tree (*Albizzia
julibrissin*)
Sweet flag (*Acorus
gramineus*)   Charm against evil

LATE SUMMER

DOMINANT
Cape jasmine
Crape-myrtle
Pomegranate   Summer solstice

SUBORDINATE
Althea
Artemisia   Charm against evil
Celosia
Hollyhock
Hosta
Lily   Harmony, brotherhood

AUTUMN

DOMINANT
  *Chrysanthemum   Friendship, longevity, nobility

SUBORDINATE
  Begonia Evansiana
  Camellia Sasanqua
  Hibiscus
  Fruit:
    Apples   A blessing
    Peaches   Longevity, immortality
    Pomegranate (ripe)   Fertility
    Sweet olive   Literary success; good luck

JAPANESE

In Japan we have the highest development of the art of arranging living plant material ever attained prior to our contemporary American era. Although very different from the Japanese, the American art has during the past decade become almost equally stylized in its own way, as well as equally, if not more, adept.

In our opinion the greatest lessons to be learned in the West from Japanese flower arrangement are the virtues of simplicity and the possibilities inherent in the most meager material *if* sensitivity and skill are used in its grooming and arrangement.

Originally the Oriental use of cut flowers was confined to temple decorations. In the sixth century a Japanese emissary to China is said to have brought back with him to Japan the custom of using fresh flowers for this purpose and it was during this period that Ikenobo, the first formal school, was developed. From that early period to modern times, Japanese flower art has had as its inspiration religious and moral symbolism. The art then spread to the nobility where it was practiced in their homes, as well as by the priesthood in the temples.

Beginning with Ikenobo, innumerable schools of arrangement have since developed, some advocating the completely formal Shin, or erect-line arrangement usually displayed in bronze containers on carved teakwood stands or taborets; the Gyo, or semiformal school which features flowing, sweeping lines in a greater variety of containers; and finally the So, or informal school where even greater freedom is acceptable, the flowers being displayed in baskets, bamboo vases, and natural wood containers as well as in pottery, on bases of bamboo or natural wood.

All styles are composed of three main elements: *Shu* (symbolizing heaven), one and one half times the height of the container (or the breadth of a wide, low dish); *Hikae* (man), two thirds the height of Shu; and *Nejime* (earth), two thirds the height of Shu. Intermediate lines, subordinate to the three main elements, are called *Chukan*.

The many Japanese schools, past and present, each practicing its own interpretation of the basic principles of Japanese flower art, all emphasize asymmetrical balance, the basic form of design being triangular.

Whatever the style or school, natural growth patterns and blooming periods are of utmost importance. Cut flowers and accessory material are placed as in nature, with buds, blooms, and foliage as they are found in growth, though groomed and pruned to present pictures of sophisticated perfection.

An excellent example of this rule may be found in any Japanese arrangement of the lotus. If open blossoms or seed pods are used, these always assume their natural positions as the tallest lines in the arrangement, even though the large, rounded forms at the apex of tall stems may appear awkward to Western eyes. On the other hand, it was from the Japanese that we learned how much more graceful and beautiful are arrangements in which buds, such as those of roses, chrysanthemums, or iris, rise above the other plant material as they are often found in nature.

Water-lilies, Japanese iris, and other aquatic materials are always placed in low, open dishes, with plenty of water visible,

Mrs. Edwin A. Duryea. First Prize

Influence of the Japanese schools of flower art is evident today in the work of American arrangers. We have ceased blindly trying to imitate them, but their spirit is evident at every flower show.

and any supplementary plants employed are of species which grow naturally in or near the water.

It will perhaps be of interest to the American student to learn that it was also from the Japanese that we realized the importance of using three dimensions in cut-flower compositions: the possibilities of a bloom or a group of material placed in profile, well back in the container, or even in reverse.

JAPANESE arrangement of the Najeire School, in which a branch or two, held at an angle within the container, gives an illusion of naturalness.

Unlike contemporary American flower art, however, many schools in Japan lean heavily on the use of one plant material alone, or on two at most, yet so cunningly arranged that their artistry is unassailable. A tree-peony bud, one partly opened flower and one full bloom, for instance, with self-foliage, is a favorite choice, as are chrysanthemums, camellias, iris, and so on. Where two materials are employed, one usually forms the main or "heaven" line, while the other gives secondary and focal interest. In some cases, the same line material is also used for "heaven" and "man," with flowers of striking color or form in the lowest, or "earth" position.

FAMOUS SCHOOLS
OF JAPANESE FLOWER ARRANGEMENT

IKENOBO (later IKEBANA), *6th Century*   Strictly formal, erect arrangements of three elements. No artificial bending or shaping was permitted. Stems were held closely together as a unit for several inches above rim of container. Ikenobo is divided into three styles:

1. SHIN, which is essentially the original formal Ikenobo. Formal bronze containers.

2. GYO, which permits greater informality, the main branches being sloped somewhat from the perpendicular. Low dishes, usubata (three-legged vases with broad lips), and bamboo vases.

3. SO, which is characterized by more freedom of line and a greater departure from the rigid perpendicular. Greater latitude in use of containers.

All three are based on the three main elements of heaven, man, and earth.

RIKKWA, *11th Century*   First created as temple offerings by a Buddhist priest, Senkei, Rikkwa compositions were pyramidal in form, symbolizing landscapes by using appropriate plant material to represent mountains, hills, valleys, and other features.

SUNAMONO RIKKWA, or SHOKWA, *15th Century*   This was a semiformal adaptation of Rikkwa developed by another priest, Senjun. He used low dishes as well as vases and introduced asymmetrical, flowing designs.

In the later development of Shokwa, the branches are held in place by a forked stick braced in the mouth of a straight-sided container as in Najeire (see below). This style also employs the three main elements, and here, too, stems are all held closely near the mouth of the container to appear as one.

NAJEIRE, *16th Century* (still popular)   Here is the most naturalistic and informal of Japanese styles, featuring one long, erect, leaning, or trailing branch one and a half to two times the height of the vase, balanced by a grouping near the rim.

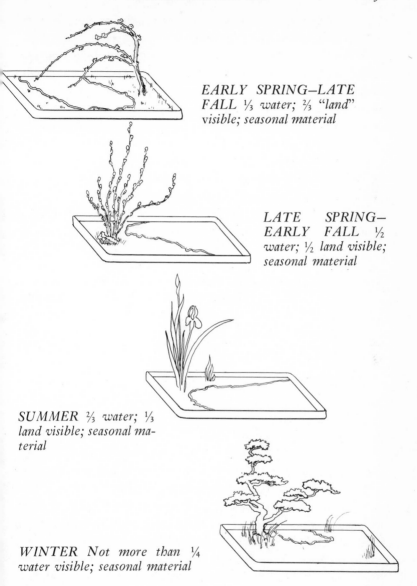

EARLY SPRING—LATE FALL ⅓ *water;* ⅔ *"land" visible; seasonal material*

LATE SPRING—EARLY FALL ½ *water;* ½ *land visible; seasonal material*

SUMMER ⅔ *water;* ⅓ *land visible; seasonal material*

WINTER *Not more than* ¼ *water visible; seasonal material*

MORIBANA—Arrangements which are replicas of natural scenes in miniature.

Great skill is required, however, to create the seemingly casual effects attained by the Japanese.

This school more nearly follows our line-mass style than any other in Japan. Here, too, forked sticks, crossed and bound sticks, or split stems are used to hold material in place, rather than the standard needle-point holders. Vases only, never low dishes, are used.

HEIKWA (modern)   Used first in the tea ceremony (see page 133), this style is similar to Najeire.

MORIBANA (1929)   This modern school derives from Rikkwa, but in Moribana, emphasis is on the natural beauty of seasonal scenes ideally presented, rather than on religious or moral symbolism. Low dishes are used with branches to represent trees; rocks and moss for islands or land; open water areas; and material such as minor bulbs or low-growing plants in the foreground. Symbolizing the four seasons, Moribana compositions are created differently in spring, summer, autumn, and winter.

Spring, early: Seasonal plant material is placed at one side of container, leaving an expanse of water covering one third its surface.

Spring, late: Seasonal plant material is placed at one side of container, an expanse of water covering one half its surface.

Summer: Seasonal plant material covers one third, water two thirds container's surface.

Autumn, early: As in late spring, but of seasonal material.

Autumn, late: As in early spring, but of seasonal material.

Winter: Seasonal plant material is placed in foreground and central portion of container, with not more than one third of its surface showing water. In midwinter, only one quarter or even one eighth open water may be visible.

Pin-point or heavy iron or zinc holders, hidden with moss, stones, or grass are used to support the taller plant material.

There is no reason why Americans cannot adapt any of these Japanese styles to Western concepts, rather than slavishly adhering to rules which have little significance for us. This is true, of course, only of arrangements made for the home or for non-competitive purposes. The arranger who enters a class for any form of Japanese flower art in a show must adhere strictly to the rules laid down in the schedule.

TEA CEREMONY

In the fifteenth century the Zen tea ceremony came into being. The priests of this religious sect advocated simplicity, austerity, and absence of all elaborate ritual in protest against luxury and elaborate décor in a period of ornate magnificence.

The special tearoom, or teahouse on the grounds of the home became a feature of the sect. Unornamented, it had plain paneled walls of beautiful natural wood, kneeling mats for the tea drinkers, and an alcove at one end to hold a wall scroll or painting and a simple flower arrangement.

Arrangements for the tea ceremony were of the utmost simplicity. A few unassuming flowers, branches, or leaves in the Najeire or Heikwa style were spontaneously arranged in a kettle, basket, gourd, or driftwood container, or in a pottery, iron, or bronze boat or other informal receptacle.

To this day the position for this arrangement during the tea ceremony is in the alcove with the decorative picture or scroll as a background. In no instance is the arrangement placed in such a way as to hide the wall decoration in any way.

Guests are sometimes asked to create a tea arrangement on the spur of the moment, thus challenging their skill and originality.

The tea ceremony is still a vital part of Japanese life. Some of the Hiroshima "maidens," who recently came to this country for plastic surgery, taught its ritual to Girl Scout troops and to groups of private- and public-school pupils in the vicinity of New York City.

11

OCCIDENTAL FLORAL ART

The influences which have helped crystallize our present-day ideals of flower arrangement are the art forms of the distant and more recent past in all parts of the world. Whether art concepts are expressed in architecture, sculpture, painting, ceramics, or designs created of actual plant material, the principles are the same. The art of any given period or civilization reflects the tastes and ideals of that time and place. Thus the sparse, formal simplicity of Oriental paintings and prints is also evident in formal Oriental arrangement. The fussy, over-crowded décor of the Victorian period is characteristic also of the floral decorations of the time; and modern arrangement has developed to enhance the uncluttered, clean-cut interiors where it is displayed.

In a comprehensive work such as this, there is space only for rather brief and condensed discussions of each of the more important eras which have contributed to contemporary art concepts.

These are planned to be of help not only in giving a broader base of understanding to the arranger of today but to give her the essential information needed to create floral designs of a given period or culture, either for exhibition work or for home use in appropriate settings.

FLOWER ART OF ANCIENT CIVILIZATIONS

EGYPT: In ancient Egypt during the years 2800 to 28 B.C., the use of flowers in religious ceremonies, for decorative purposes in the home, and for personal adornment was a highly important aspect of the culture of the land.

Flowers were so abundant that they were even shipped to Rome. Water-lilies, lotus, acacia, roses, violets, Madonna lilies, narcissus, jasmine, and poppies were among the species commonly grown and used as cut flowers. Fruits, vines, and foliage were equally popular.

Our knowledge of Egyptian flower art comes, of course, from the tombs where paintings, enamels, bas-reliefs, jewelry, and even actual plant material have been made available for study by the excavations of archaeologists. From these we learn that, whether placed in bowls—the containers commonly used —or formed into head wreaths, garlands, or collars for presentation to guests, bright-hued, fragrant flowers, berries, and leaves were disposed in regimented rows (not overlapped), the colors sharply segregated.

Formal bouquets, as offerings to the gods or to the dead, were of lotus flowers combined with other fruits, blossoms, and foliage.

Fruits and vegetables, neatly piled in low baskets, were formed into mounded designs topped by lotus blossoms and edged by a symmetrical row of lotus petals or leaves. These were served at feasts and used as temple offerings.

Many of the plants used had symbolic meanings for the Egyptians. The fig symbolized the fertility of the valley of the Nile. The ivy was sacred to Osiris, judge of the underworld and god of agriculture, arts, and crafts. Above all, the lotus, together with marsh grasses, was a part of the ritual when interceding with the gods for rain.

Existing containers of ancient Egypt, on display in museums, include low bowls of glass, pottery, and bronze, some with built-in flower holders, and baskets and fruit dishes on pedestals not unlike our fruit compotes of the Victorian era.

GREECE: In ancient Greece (600 to 146 B.C., flowers were not arranged in vases or other containers nor in bouquets, if we may judge by existing records, but were a part of religious rituals, being strewn on the ground during festivals and

Mrs. Chester S. Cook

A fruit arrangement in the manner of a Roman mosaic.

A massed period arrangement by the same artist, in a container suggestive of the Renaissance which produced Benvenuto Cellini and other superb goldsmiths.

made into garlands and wreaths which were worn at such times.

Flower wreaths took the place in Greek life of our flower arrangements. Wreaths were placed on the brows of living heroes and on statues of gods, goddesses, and famous mortals. Grape leaves and fruit were sacred to Dionysius, iris to Adonis, laurel to Apollo, and roses to Aphrodite.

Garlands fashioned of roses, sweet marjoram, lilies, hyacinths, iris, narcissus, and violets were sent as funeral flowers and employed to decorate graves. Wreaths of flowers, fruit, and leaves sacred to Dionysius were borne in on trays at banquets given in his honor, and garlands of fresh flowers decorated the tables on which baskets of fresh fruits and vegetables were also featured.

Lovers fashioned for each other fragrant wreaths and garlands of violets, thyme, narcissus, berries, or seed pods, the blooms being all of uniform size, interspersed with leaves.

So important a place did wreaths and garlands hold in ancient Greek culture that pot plants were grown indoors by many families to supply the necessary plant material. Florists were also engaged to make them as gifts and as decorations for special occasions, much as present-day American florists make sprays for funerals and arrangements for presents and home decoration.

Fruits, vegetables, and flowers, beautifully arranged according to the fashion of the times in baskets or upright horns of plenty, were proffered in solemn ritual to the gods in temple services, the sacred plant of each immortal being featured in his or her offerings.

ROME: Imperial Rome (28 B.C. to 325 A.D.) created little that was new in the use of fresh flowers, but rather embraced the earlier customs of Greece, and as her own civilization became more luxurious and effete, elaborated the use of fresh plant material to overpowering proportions.

Flowers and fruits arranged in low baskets, much as we might make mass compositions today, were carried to the banquet tables where guests were crowned and draped with massive floral wreaths and garlands, and where fresh cut roses lay like deep carpets on the floor and were dropped from the ceiling in a rain of extravagant color and fragrance.

Temple offerings in baskets and cornucopias were used also, but the arrangement was heavier and less graceful than those of the Greeks.

BYZANTIUM: The Eastern Roman Empire (325 to 600 A.D.), which escaped the rape of the Goths and Vandals because it was located in Byzantium on the Bosporus, developed a technique in floral art preserved for us by the church mosaics in Ravenna and elsewhere.

Even a glance at these symmetrical, stylized compositions is enough to tell us that here is the inspiration for many modern artificial Christmas "trees" as well as for much contemporary display material.

Beautiful urns, chalices, and handled bowls of bronze, precious metals, glass, and semiprecious stones, such as porphyry and jade, were filled with completely symmetrical, spirelike foliage "trees" built to tapering tips and decorated at regular intervals with clusters of flowers or fruits in pure jewel colors.

Another style was characterized by a central stem rising from a low container, with pairs of flowers, leaves, or fruits bound to it, at set intervals on either side, in perfect, even balance, making a sort of artificial plant tapering to the top and composed of a series of exotic twin elements such as anthuriums, ginger blossoms, or clusters of pepper or pyracantha berries, again in bright, clear colors.

Tall containers were filled with fans of tropical foliage, flanked by bunches of grapes or other fruit clusters drooping over the wide lip at each side. Here, too, we can find the inspiration for our present-day placement of grapes in fruit arrangements in stemmed compotes.

Formal bouquets used as church offerings were slim and cone-shaped. Here the flowers and/or leaves were bound tightly about a stick, forming symmetrical tiers similar to the stiffly bound bouquets of blossoms and leaves made even today in Mexico.

PERSIA: Beginning in the fourteenth century, Persian art

begins to depict arrangements of flowers in Oriental containers.

Short-stemmed blossoms were arranged in symmetrical balance, topped by a tall-stemmed lily, iris, or rose. Branches of flowering shrubs were also made into one-flower bouquets. Some containers appearing in works of Persian art up to the beginning of the eighteenth century had openings rather like those of a strawberry jar in which accessory plant material was placed.

Colors were varied, less intense than in Byzantine flower art, but beautifully blended and contrasted as in Persian rugs. Tulips, narcissus, and other bulbous flowers were favored, if we may judge by surviving works of art. Chinese porcelain containers, bronze or brass ewers and vases, and pottery flasks and jars were used.

THE MIDDLE AGES: During medieval times (476 to 1400 A.D.), after the fall of the western Roman Empire and before the beginning of the Renaissance, little is known of flower art until the thirteenth century, which ushered in the Gothic period. During this era, flowers, foliage, and fruits were freely used in ornamentation of the great thirteenth-century cathedrals. There are also still extant tapestries, paintings, and illuminated manuscripts of the fourteenth and fifteenth centuries which show tall vases containing a few long-stemmed flowers, and the making and presentation of wreaths, garlands, and baskets of flowers. As the rose, lily, and columbine were sacred to the Virgin, these species often appeared in works of art representing the Annunciation.

Taken as a whole, however, this is the period in Europe about which we know least. With the exception of a possible class in Gothic at a flower show where exhibitors are experienced and skillful, it is unlikely that the average arranger will be called upon to do work with cut flowers in any of the styles current during those dark and obscure ages of history.

THE RENAISSANCE: With the beginning of the Renaissance (1400 to 1600), which spread from Italy through the rest of Europe, there came into being a new impetus in all the arts, a coalescence and revitalization of the many classical styles

heretofore described. Such artists as Cellini and Holbein created
precious vases, Byzantine in inspiration.

Bouquets of formal balance were made in choice urns,
chalices, and bowls. These appear often, in Renaissance paintings, set on the floor, a window sill, or a high shelf. Botticelli's
paintings show very tall arrangements, especially of lilies and
roses sacred to the Virgin, and narrow-necked vases with flar-
ing mouths holding one twisted candle surrounded by short-
stemmed roses. Tight, formal bouquets or light, airy flowers
such as lilies-of-the-valley, pinks, and daisies appear in low
bowls and baskets.

Wreaths and garlands, preserved for us in the works of the
Della Robbias, Raphael, Fra Filippo Lippi, and Fra Angelico
came to the height of perfection during this period. Fruits,
cones, berries, and foliage, as well as flowers, were used to
create lovely designs which are widely copied today, especially for Christmas decorations. Colors were brilliant and
mixed, with no studied harmonies.

Venetian glass, fine enamel, precious metals, beautifully
glazed potteries, and later blown glass were used for containers;
and shapes varied from urns, bowls, and jars to epergnes,
pitchers, ewers, and tall, wide-lipped vases.

In studying Renaissance paintings which include cut flowers,
the student is immediately impressed by the fact that here, for
the first time, natural placements can often be found, tall stems
rising gracefully from the containers, uncrowded and permitted to display their own natural beauty of form and color.

BAROQUE: Starting in Italy in the late sixteenth century
and spreading gradually throughout Europe, the Baroque style
of art, decoration, and architecture developed. The period ex-
tends from about 1550 to 1760, having its inception toward the
close of the Renaissance. Michelangelo is credited with inspir-
ing this extravagant décor, and some of his followers carried
its ornate boldness so far that it fell into a general disrepute
from which it has only recently emerged.

Flower artists abounded, especially in Holland and Flanders,
producing paintings executed in massed but rhythmic, asym-

metrical balance, especially the *S*, or Hogarthian curve, named after William Hogarth, the English painter who declared in his *Analysis of Beauty*, written in 1753, that it was "the line of beauty." Rich in horticultural detail, the floral paintings of the period were large and lavish, with many accessories, varying from bird's nests, butterflies, and bees to figurines, jewels, and fans. In France, delicate, airy compositions were the mode, full of rhythmic motion and, like much contemporary flower art, as greatly dependent for their effects on the "voids" as on the plant material itself.

Now, for the first time in great houses, niches were especially designed to hold vases and urns of cut flowers. At large functions table decorations of flowers were placed in epergnes set at intervals down the center of the board. Smaller arrangements were a regular part of the décor of all elegant rooms.

Colors were rich and dark, or subdued, with occasional light areas; and containers were heavy urns, jugs, bowls, and vases in metal, glass, or stone. In France elaborately painted and decorated porcelain was popular.

ROCOCO: An offshoot of Baroque art were the Rococo (rock and shell) forms freely used by Baroque artists during the reign of Louis XV of France. Rococo art (1715 to 1774) spread from France to other parts of Europe where it was exemplified by its gay, light, asymmetrical designs and fanciful motifs of shells, scrolls, foliage, and flowers.

Like the airy, silk costumes of the French court and the intimate, overdecorated feminine rooms of the period, Rococo flower art was more delicate in color and design than the Baroque. To the large showy blossoms in mass compositions were added frail, trailing vines, such as honeysuckle and morning-glory, and slender-stemmed small blooms like columbine, carnations, cornflowers, daisies, and pansies. Fern fronds, Christmas-roses, larkspurs, lilacs, and other flowering shrubs were much used.

Instead of the dominant Hogarthian curve of the Baroque style, Rococo arrangements, like other art designs of the time, were characterized by short, shell-like spiral curves and scrolls, the individual flower heads nodding on dainty, curving stems.

Small arrangements, too, were common—a few blossoms and buds on a side table in a little china vase or shell dish are usually to be seen in portraits of ladies in their boudoirs.

Intricately decorated porcelain vases, small shells, and leaf-shaped forms gilded and mounted on decorative bases, epergnes urns, baskets, wall pockets, cornucopias, fan-shaped china containers made up of five separate bottlelike vases joined at the base, and many other types were created especially for cut flowers. As the Chinese influence was strong at this time in Europe, eighteenth-century Chinese containers, backgrounds, screens, lacquered tables, and similar art objects were also popular.

The china figurines of the eighteenth century, so much cherished by antique collectors today, were especially created for use as accessories on the elaborately decorated banquet tables where epergnes and stemmed dishes were placed at intervals, filled with flowers, foliage, and fruit. The buffet table too, came to its greatest elegance during this time, being decorated with garlands of foliage, flowers, and pyramids of fruit, the whole lit by dozens of candles in ornate candelabra. Colors were pale and delicate like the porcelains, paintings, and other works of art of the day.

When the Rococo style finally reached England, it was developed with more dignity and less airiness than in France. It did, however, bring lighter colors into popularity, and the décor in general became less massive and overpowering.

ENGLISH GEORGIAN: Flower artists of the early Georgian period in England (which extended from 1714 to 1760) were Flemish or Dutch rather than English. In their many ample flower paintings, a mass of seasonal material is crammed into a wide-lipped, low urn, with little regard for design.

In one of Peter Casteel's works, the twisted stems and bizarre blooms of Fantasy tulips rise boldly to a height almost twice that of their container, while primulas, hyacinths, branches of flowering shrubs, Oriental poppies, daffodils, and other blooms casually fill the space to overflowing, with curving stems and

These 3 Trees Flower'd at the Earle of Pembrokes.

The Yellow Tulip Tree at 12 Years old in the year 1720. it bore above 300 Tulips.
The White Tulip with 4 Fibers, grows the best ever green with an Aromatic Smel, flower'd in 4 years; but never grows near so big as the other Tulip tree.
The Silke Cotton Tree, flower'd small parts very beautifull out of the Green Pods the white, not as the Linnen Cotton but brittle, turning
as Silke, the Cotton when all expanded out of one of these little Pods takes so much room a large Walnut the inchers Silk Cotton tree a tree not so big flower'd large

Robert Furber, "Furber Gardner over against high Parke Gate
near Kingsinton," executed this hand-colored engraving of "Tulip
Tree and Magnolia and Silke Cotton Tree, blossoms arranged in
an urn," during the first half of the eighteenth century. His
"Twelve Months of Flowers," London 1730, and "Twelve Months
of Fruit," London 1732, are equally well-known examples of floral
decorations of the Georgian period.

*FLEMISH
PERIOD*

*Arrangement by Mrs.
Anne Elizabeth Erhorn*

*CLASSIC
REVIVAL*

*Arrangement by Mrs. John H.
Squires, Jr.*

VICTORIAN PERIOD

Arrangement by Mrs. Anne Elizabeth Erborn

FRENCH INFLUENCE

Arrangement by Mrs. Dexter M. Ferry, Jr.

nodding blooms. A flower or two lie on the table, and while the observer is charmed by the soft, rich blending of color and the virtuosity with which each petal and leaf is executed, the over-all effect is rather like that of a Medusa's head. Jacob Van Huysam showed more restraint and, with a fine sense of design, posed his galaxy of mixed blossoms against large, dark foliage masses or drew the eye to a focal center of exquisite pale flowers by flanking them with dark blooms.

Massive urns, handled cups, bough pots (sturdy, oblong "pots," or jars in which boughs and branches were customarily arranged in summer in the unused fireplaces) wall vases, elaborate epergnes, and baskets were used, as well as eighteenth-century Chinese vases. Materials were porcelain, English china, bronze, and silver.

NEOCLASSICISM: During the last half of the eighteenth century and the first third of the nineteenth, in Europe, Great Britain, and America, a revival of classic architecture, decoration, and furnishings took place. This may have been a natural reaction to the Baroque and Rococo periods which immediately preceded it.

These were the times (late Georgian and Regency in Great Britain) of the Adams brothers, Sheraton, Hepplewhite, Chippendale, Josiah Wedgwood.

In France the décor of Louis XVI, the Directoire and Empire periods marked a gradual change from delicate fragility to the massive, overdecorated style favored by Napoleon.

In America, the Federal period of the young republic saw the designs of Charles Bulfinch, Thomas Jefferson, Alexander Hamilton, and Duncan Phyfe develop a chaste elegance all its own.

During this time of new classicism, the garland and the wreath regained much of their ancient Greek and Roman prestige. These motifs were much used in tapestries, wallpapers, bas-reliefs, and other objects. Wreaths of symbolic plant material were again worn and carried in the old classic tradition by people of fashion.

There seems to have been little direct emphasis on arranging flowers, as few records have come down to us in paintings or other art works of bouquets actually in use as decorations for new classic interiors. There were flower painters like Jean Louis Prevost and Pierre Joseph Redonte, and floral motifs were much used in fabrics, carvings, and wallpapers.

There was a wide choice of containers, from the epergne, which survived from the Baroque period, to five-fingered holders, classic urns, vases, wall vases, cornucopias, tole ware vases, silver dishes, boats, and baskets. Chinese containers were still in vogue, and Wedgwood was busy creating his urns and vases decorated with troops of classic figures.

During the early part of the period, colors were as cool and muted as "Williamsburg blue" walls, in spacious, uncluttered interiors which, thanks to the Rockefellers' restorations in Williamsburg, Virginia, are so familiar to Americans. Plain or striped hangings, sometimes edged with gold, were preferred to flowered fabrics.

Later, during the Empire period, heavy brocaded hangings and much carved furniture became the mode; and to blend with these, containers took on added weight—bronze, ceramic, or alabaster urns with thick stems and heavy bases, bough pots and massive vases and compotes. Material was massed in symmetrical balance, but with the lighter touch of some delicate flower sprays tucked in among the heavier blooms.

EARLY AMERICAN: There are sparse records of the use of cut flowers in America from 1620 to the middle of the eighteenth century.

We may reasonably assume that the rigid religious discipline of the Pilgrims and the Massachusetts Bay Colony could have considered the use of bouquets for house decoration as an unforgivable worldly vanity. But we do know that slips, roots, and seeds of English garden flowers found their way to New England among the chattels of the settlers and were soon established in the dooryards of Massachusetts homes.

It is reasonable to suppose that if cut flowers were ever permitted in the primitive homes of the early settlers, they must have been placed in homely containers dedicated to more utilitarian uses: pitchers, bowls, pots, and jars of earthenware, pewter, or wood, for the worldly goods brought over on those first sailing ships must have been pitiably few.

In the more luxurious colonies of Virginia and Maryland, and even in Quaker Pennsylvania and Dutch New York, elegant vases, urns, and epergnes, delft, pottery, and stoneware jars were among the treasurers brought from Great Britain and Holland. By the middle of the eighteenth century, the China trade was bringing in Lowestoft and other Oriental porcelains. Silver was being imported and also being made by fine craftsmen in this country. Bough pots, bowls, cache pots, epergnes, jardinieres, jugs, urns, vases, and baskets made of earthenware, pottery, tole, pewter, and silver were in use. The late eighteenth century saw the importation and home manufacture of glass as well.

The simple garden flowers of the period included anemones, lilies, and roses, together with the Dutch bulbs and old-fashioned perennials like hollyhocks, phlox, and violets, and annuals such as bachelor's buttons, marigolds, and everlastings. Dried flowers were employed to relieve winter interiors.

Since we do not really know how these materials were arranged, except for a very few examples of vases of flowers appearing on side tables in early American portraits, we must judge that they were simply placed in mass bouquets, following the general outlines of the British and European styles of the same period but probably arranged with less sophistication.

NINETEENTH CENTURY GREAT BRITAIN

VICTORIAN: After all this severity and pomposity, it is small wonder that the nineteenth century brought with it a backward swing to romanticism and a fussy coziness which reached its peak in Great Britain under the reign of Victoria.

Rooms were replete with heavy, dark embossed wallpapers, plush or velvet upholstered rosewood and mahogany furniture, weighty figured damask hangings. Favorite colors were dark greens, rich reds and browns, with figured rugs and carpets and somber paintings in massive gold frames.

Also popular were alabaster urns and vases, much decorated and elaborately hand-painted vases of porcelain from Sèvres and Limoges; silver or pewter and glass epergnes were filled to overflowing with roses, tulips, lilies, pansies, anemones, dahlias, fuchsias, asters, and other garden flowers. Stems were comparatively short, the bouquets usually being approximately the height of the container, but weeping or drooping lines of flowering vines, weeping willow, bleeding heart, and other materials with sentimental connotations were used to relieve the monotony of outline. These materials, characteristic of this age of sentimentality and romance, should be included in any modern composition arranged in the Victorian manner.

Used in much the same way were pressed Sandwich glass (manufactured on Cape Cod) and unglazed white Parian ware (made in Bennington, Vermont), as well as Chinese ginger jars, other Oriental imports, and containers imported from France and England.

Not content with living flowers, Victorian ladies made bouquets and wreaths of bead and wax flowers, which were preserved under glass domes or in heavy frames. These were among the "artistic horrors" of an age noted for its lack of taste, judged by contemporary standards.

It was in the Victorian period that the nosegay and the tussy mussy reached their top popularity. Ladies of fashion assembled these small, fragrant bouquets with great care and carried them to social functions and to church, where the tightly laced Victorian damsels sniffed them to revive themselves when overcome by sudden, but understandable, faintness. These little nosegays still have charm and are often created by modern arrangers who place them in appropriate containers, such as china hands or small cornucopias of glass or china.

NINETEENTH CENTURY FRANCE

France, during the nineteenth century, escaped the stultify-ing influence of Victorianism which had Great Britain and America in its grip.

In this century, the artists of France rose to such great heights and created so much that was new and original that few periods in the history of the world can compare with it in creativity.

ROMANTICISM: Beginning with the great romanticists like Eugene Delacroix and other lesser lights such as Gustave Courbet and the primitive painter Henri Rousseau, still lifes of flowers and fruits were beautifully and sensitively rendered, following the early traditions of the seventeenth century when French flower painting became an important part of the inte-rior décor. The nineteenth century, however, even during the earlier romantic years, displayed greater vigor, originality, and naturalism. Men like Bonnard, Fantin-Latour, and Redon left behind them flower paintings of great beauty.

Later, the great Impressionists—Degas, Monet, Renoir, Cézanne, and Van Gogh—while they were creating a com-pletely new school of art, added invaluable examples of flower and fruit painting to the art treasures of the world. Each painted in his own individual style, but each with remarkable vigor and originality.

It is to these geniuses that we must look for French trends in flower arrangement during the nineteenth century. Mass compositions of flowers; tables bearing vases of blossoms, bowls of fruit, and open blooms tossed carelessly on the cloth; jars of mixed garden flowers, simply arranged; still lifes including a jar of flowers with other objects in the design—whatever the subject, the execution is full of light and soft, yet brilliant, color.

More arrangements and compositions in current flower shows, in the manner of the nineteenth-century French paint-

Mrs. Charles C. Whitlock

This contemporary arrangement in the French manner shows how we can adapt period containers and styles to current usage.

ers, would, in our opinion, do a great deal more for the creative inspiration of the modern arranger than struggling to reproduce the tight and trite flower styles of Victorian or even Georgian England.

EARLY TWENTIETH CENTURY
IN EUROPE AND AMERICA

At the close of the nineteenth century and during the first decade of the twentieth, the New Art, or Art Nouveau forced from Great Britain and America the overcrowded, stuffy décor of Victorianism. The accent of Art Nouveau was on naturalism, pastel colors, and rhythmic forms. Though not particularly admired today, the decorative objects which came to the fore during this time represented a distinct improvement over those of the immediate past.

This was the day of scrim window curtains, stenciled in natural colors with tall, graceful cattails or with running vines; of Japanese wallpapers, screens, and art objects; and of European- and American-made vases and decorative objects, simple and rhythmic in form and decorated in an entirely new manner.

Containers of the period include the now precious Tiffany and Lalique glass vases, the former in rich opalescent colors and unusual shapes, the latter of heavy, clear glass, etched and decorated. Dull-surfaced jars, bowls, and vases of pottery, French porcelain, heavy glass, and metal were freely decorated with naturalistic floral patterns or with birds and butterflies.

Flowers placed in these containers were comparatively few, not really "arranged" at all, but rather gathered in the hand, then set in the vase. This was before the days of flower holders, and most bouquets were in tall vases, the flowers about the same height as the container, or even less. Paintings of the French artist Redon are characteristic of the floral art of this era in colors, placement of material, and types of containers.

It was during this period also, due to Western recognition of Japanese art, that line "arrangements" of flowering shrubs began to be set in lower dishes and in Oriental bowls. Lacking in design, these were, nevertheless, a forerunner of the Western interest in Japanese flower arrangement soon to develop.

12

CONTEMPORARY FLOWER ARRANGEMENT

Arrangement today in America is constantly changing. This is natural and healthy for any living art. Because it is so very much alive, with so many artists devoted to it, there are many differing schools of thought, and each year brings new trends and fashions.

In general, however, we may say that arrangement today falls into three categories:

> Contemporary Mass Arrangement
> Contemporary Line Arrangement
> Contemporary Line-mass Arrangement

In addition to the creation of floral designs in these three categories, a considerable amount of show work is done in reproducing the floral arts of other times. We call this Period Arrangement (see Chapters 10 and 11). Many beautiful compositions in this field are created at every show, but we cannot consider it as a contemporary art form. Artists, in making period arrangements, strive to reproduce—and sometimes to improve upon—a style of floral art from some past period. Much study and research goes into period arrangement. Authentic containers and accessories are prerequisite, and flowers of the period, too, must be chosen for the design.

CONTEMPORARY MASS ARRANGEMENT

Modern mass designs fit into any one of the basic art forms. A mass creation may be cylindrical, pyramidal, cone-shaped, spherical, or ovoid.

In this type of arrangement, however, the entire area of the

Mrs. Samuel F. Newkirk

CONTEMPORARY MASS: An example in which many flowers are used, but with less of the overcrowding characteristic of earlier periods and with more attention to design.

design is filled with plant material. Unlike most of the mass bouquets of the past, compositions of today have:

1. A definite color harmony which may be monochromatic, analogous, or complementary (see Chapter 9).
2. Segregation of color, with gradual transition from one value to another.
3. Good balance, either symmetrical or asymmetrical.
4. A strong focal point of massed plant material.
5. Less dense material to give graceful height and breadth.
6. Emphasis on repetition, contrast, and texture.

Containers should be large and heavy enough to hold the material comfortably and to give a feeling of adequate support.

Large blooms (such as peonies, full-blown roses, tulips, and the like) may be combined with more airy blossoms (such as lilac, stocks, bulbous iris, freesias, and narcissus) to give contrast in size, form, and texture.

Modern mass arrangements, while creating an effect of abundance, should not be so exuberant as to be overpowering, as were the mass still lifes of the old Dutch and Flemish painters.

CONTEMPORARY LINE ARRANGEMENT

Though less popular today than it was a few decades ago when Japanese flower art was sweeping this country, line arrangement is still a living part of contemporary floral design.

Undoubtedly our present form of line composition owes much to Oriental precepts, yet it is more free and untrammeled, giving the artist an opportunity to exercise her originality, imagination, and ingenuity.

Sometimes when viewing show arrangements, I feel that only in the line work can modern-arrangement artists abandon their designs to the natural beauty of the plant material, employing its natural curves and forms rather than contriving to rearrange them into something as unlike living, growing flowers as is the average Easter hat.

A modern MASS ARRANGEMENT *showing many and varied flowers, but with colors segregated and a distinct center of interest, as contrasted to period mass arrangements.*

Mrs. Dunham C. Jones   *Mrs. J. B. Goldsmith*

(Left) A modern LINE ARRANGEMENT *emphasizing rhythmic lines and silhouette, but with depth only at the focal point.*
(Right) The modern LINE-MASS ARRANGEMENT *(as the flower-show schedules designate it) is a nice combination of emphasis on each of the two. Here repetition and gradation help dramatize the focal center and create a Hogarthian curve.*

Basically, line arrangement is floral design created entirely of lines and the silhouettes of individual leaves and/or flowers. These, *and the voids between them,* form the design. This does not mean, however, that line compositions are two-dimensional. Branches, stems, or other materials are placed in overlapping planes to assure depth, so that the eye may be carried back into space as well as upward and to the left and right.

Symmetrical line compositions for modern interiors are often built around a central figurine or other accessory which provides the focal center and dictates the type of plant material forming the line design about it.

Asymmetrical line arrangements are more popular as they

Mrs. Audrey H. Dunn

PURE LINE: *A prize-winning line arrangement of dried twigs and orchids, showing the influence of Japanese flower art. (Looks easy, doesn't it? Just wait until you try it yourself!)*

give more scope for freedom and originality. They may be created of heavy material such as magnolia or pine branches, or of delicate grasses, vines, or thin-stemmed flowers like salpiglossis. In the latter type, graceful curves and sweeping lines give a feeling of rhythmic movement which is hard to match in any other sort of composition.

A fine clear-cut design, be it a Hogarthian curve, a spiral, a crescent, a horizontal line or curve, an *L* or *V* form, is the only positive requirement for a contemporary line arrangement. It is sometimes hard to say where the line arrangement ceases and the line-mass begins, but in general we may state that when even a small area of massed material is added for focal interest, the division between the two has been crossed.

CONTEMPORARY LINE-MASS ARRANGEMENT

In America today a type of arrangement has evolved, as stylized in its way as the classic flower art of Japan. Though very different, contemporary line-mass arrangement in this country owes much to Oriental precepts.

Clean-cut, sculptural design is of the utmost importance, with equal emphasis on the skeletal pattern of lines which determines the general shape of the arrangement, on the voids between the lines and other plant forms, and on the massed material which gives it weight, focal interest, emphasis, and depth.

We hear and read much about the basic forms into which all compositions must fall whether they be paintings, sculpture, or other types of artistic expression. The art teacher asks her pupils to find the triangles or other basic designs upon which masterpieces of the past and present are conceived and executed. The well-landscaped garden, or even the pool which may be one of its features, has its basic form.

If you have an inborn sense of design, your arrangements will naturally be fitted into an imaginary basic art form such

Mrs. Nelson B. Grove

LINE-MASS: An arrangement emphasizing the bold silhouette (triangular in form) characteristic of Oriental arrangement, but having greater depth and more lavish employment of flowers and foliage.

The THREE-DIMENSIONAL, *or arrangement in depth is distinct in that it moves back in space, giving the effect of a piece of sculpture rather than a painting.*

as the cube, pyramid, cone, sphere, ellipsoid, cylinder, or into some part of one of these or a combination of more than one. Any of the triangular forms may be carved out of a pyramid. The partial sphere, crescent, or Hogarthian curve are all derived from the sphere itself, to give a few examples. (See also Chapter 7.)

In line-mass arrangement, the line portion of the design is suggested by stems, branches, or a series of blooms or leaves which inevitably lead the eye along from one end to the other. These lines, with the individual flowers, leaves, and the voids created between them form the skeletal pattern of the design. The mass portion, placed low around the main axis (see diagram, page 83), forms the center of interest and also provides balance and color. The mass design, heaviest at the edge of the container and around the focal point, becomes less dense toward its outer edges where the line design takes over, thus, by means of *transition* and *gradation*, effecting a gradual change from mass to line.

FLORAL DESIGNS IN THREE DIMENSIONS

Probably the strongest trend in arrangement today is the emphasis currently being given to *depth*. The object of the artist is to make her composition move backward and forward in space by giving it sculptural depth.

In earlier books and in this volume, when discussing the principles of design (Chapter 7), we have spoken of the square, the rectangle, the triangle, the circle, and so on as basic art forms. To be strictly factual, however, in the three-dimensional art of flower arrangement we should substitute the terms sphere, cube, cylinder, pyramid, and ellipsoid because we know perfectly well that all the elements with which we work are solids. What the judges used to call "paper-doll arrangements" (too thin and flimsy for beauty) are no longer a problem because arrangers for some years now have been alerted to the importance of giving to any composition *depth* proportionate to its height and breadth.

This is accomplished by presenting one or more elements (groups of plant material, flowers, or individual leaves) in profile or even in reverse.

Large foliage which is naturally rather flat, such as canna, aspidistra, and dracaena, is rolled or turned at an angle to show part of the reverse side. Staggered one behind the other, these rolled or turned leaves create an impression of considerable depth. (See illustration page 52.)

Square, oblong, or oval containers are sometimes placed diagonally in the display area to give a feeling of *moving back*. The arrangement, of course, faces the observer but is built up well with the taller material toward the rear to give further perspective; or a pair of containers is used, placed diagonally one behind the other, again with the taller lines of the design at the back.

In striving toward *depth*, many arrangers today are producing work which has the weight and massiveness of modern sculpture. Sturdy, often massive containers, heavy foliage, and accessory material such as cypress knees, large pieces of driftwood, rocks, burls, and burl bases are preferred. With these are placed fruits, vegetables, large cones and seed pods, ceramics, carvings, sculpture. In such compositions there are often very few flowers, or no flowers at all. Those which are present— Calla-lilies, ginger blossoms, strelitzias, and the like—are seldom arranged in a naturalistic manner but become parts of a sculptural design reminiscent of the garlands and other carved motifs which were characteristic of Roman architectural decoration and the Classic Revival.

It is hardly too much to say that the devotees of this form of composition create not flower arrangements but sculptural designs made up of an assortment of objects, sometimes including living plant material.

Many of these compositions are masterful in conception and execution and make distinctive decorations, especially for modern interiors, but are they flower arrangements in the true sense of the word? Do they give any scope to featuring the unstudied charm which characterizes the natural growth habits of many flowers?

It is an undeniable fact that there are always current trends and fashions in arrangement, just as there are in costume design, painting, or any other form of expression. We have only to study the history of Japanese flower arrangement to realize fully how ironbound with tradition and practice such an art form can become, and how the work and teachings of each new master outmode the precepts of previous oracles. Are we, as a nation of flower arrangers, following in their footsteps?

Each flower artist must decide this question for herself. We would like to suggest, however, to that dedicated group of women—the certified judges who labor so faithfully in the vineyard—the advisability of a refresher course every year or two, not so much to brush up on the latest trends in America as to analyze such trends, to study them critically as flower lovers and as artists, with a view to throwing the tremendous weight of their influence on the side of freedom, originality, and creativity, rather than on the side of slavish adherence to any one mode of the moment.

13

CLASSES OF ARRANGEMENTS
TABLE ARRANGEMENTS

In planning floral decorations for dinner, luncheon, or supper tables, the following matters must be carefully considered before selecting flowers, containers, or accessories:

1. The cloth or table mats and napkins

    a. Color
    b. Texture
    c. Quality

2. The place plates, if any
    a. Color
    b. Pattern
    c. Quality

3. Other china or pottery, glassware, and so on
    a. Color
    b. Pattern
    c. Quality
    d. Weight
    e. Texture

Flower arrangements, or compositions should be harmonious with the table setting. Colors may blend or may contrast, in one of the complementary color harmonies (see page 111). Containers and accessories should not only be a unified part of the floral design but should be chosen with the elegance or simplicity of the setting in mind.

Table arrangements fall into three main categories:

1. Those placed in the center of a table with guests seated on both sides or all around the board.

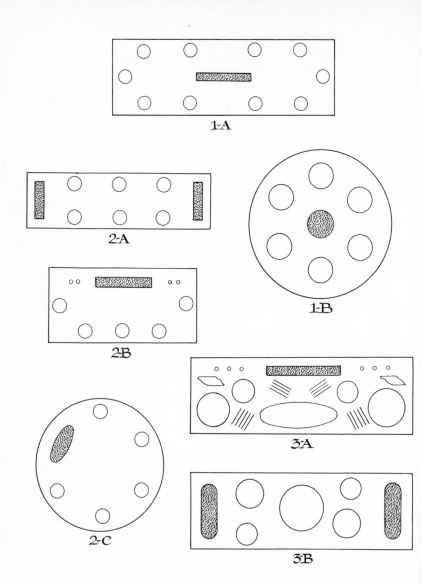

TABLE SETTINGS

(*1–A*) *Arrangement in center of oblong table.* (*1–B*) *Arrangement in center of round table.* (*2–A*) *Arrangements at ends of oblong table.* (*2–B*) *Arrangement at one side of oblong table.* (*2–C*) *Arrangement on side of round table.* (*3–A*) *Buffet arrangement, rear center; table against wall.* (*3–B*) *Buffet arrangements at ends of table against wall or free standing.*

2. Those placed at the ends or at one side of a table (see diagram, page 166).

3. Those designed for buffet tables where no one is seated, but where food and table service are displayed and where food and beverages are served.

In the first category we may be decorating for breakfast, luncheon, dinner, or supper, and the range is from absolute informality, where a pitcher or bowl of annuals brightens the family table, to a strictly formal dinner with floral decoration an important part of the general décor.

There are two limitations, however, which apply to every arrangement in this category, whether the table be oblong, square, or round: (1) the arrangement must be constructed to be viewed and enjoyed from all sides; (2) it must be below chin level of diners sitting across from each other with the flowers between them. Otherwise, guests may well be facing a bunch of flowers instead of a fellow conversationalist. If the design requires it, one tall line or two, to give height, will not obstruct the view (see diagram, page 245).

A long table calls for a central decoration longer than its width, in proportion to the shape of the board, while a round or square table demands an arrangement of similar proportions. Of course a square dish in the center of a round table, and vice versa, often provides pleasing contrast.

The fact that the "centerpiece" was viewed from all sides led to the old-fashioned custom of filling a round dish with a mass of flowers, all with stems of equal height and placed without thought of design.

Today the usual method is to place line material in a container where it can be observed from all sides and then make two, if necessary even four, small groupings, or floral designs to provide centers of interest. These are popped in where needed, at the focal points, so that the arrangement is complete from each angle viewed (see diagram page 245).

EXAMPLE 1. For the center of a refectory table, a shallow, oblong dish is used. Branches of gnarled pine, yew, juniper,

Table by Mrs. John H. Squires, Jr.

Flower and fruit decorations give wide scope for the arranger to employ originality. In the table above, the usual annoying hedge effect of a large centerpiece has been avoided by placing decorations at the ends.

Buffet by Mrs. Chester S. Cook

A subdued and harmonious, yet exciting composition with a wall wreath of dried pods and berries supported by fresh fruits and foliage on the buffet itself.

manzanita, blueberry, or spring-flowering shrubs are used as line material. Two short-stemmed designs of minor spring bulbs (one of crocus and scillas; the other of species tulips and primulas) are made up separately, the stems bound together with raffia. One is placed on each side of the main stem, covering the needle-point holder and forming a focal point for each side.

EXAMPLE 2. Spike flowers like stock, *Salvia farinacea*, lupine, or snapdragons establish the long lines of a crescent in a shallow round bowl for a round or square table. These first lines are planned to be viewed and to be plainly visible from all sides, as are also the round forms of medium height which go in next: blue lace-flower, scabiosa, small dahlias, roses, and so on.

Each of the two sides is now finished by placing short-stemmed, fully opened flowers near focal points to form centers of interest. Some of these and some foliage peep over the bowl's rim. A few short-stemmed blooms, with supplementary foliage, are also placed on the remaining two sides near the water level, tucked in close to the bases of the line material.

When completed, this makes a low arrangement, with adequate line design, but pleasing from every angle because centers of interest are visible from all sides.

Fruits and/or vegetables on a suitable tray, often combined with flowers and foliage, with accessories such as ceramic birds or figurines for added interest, and flanked by candles in suitable sticks or candelabra make striking designs for dinner-table centers (see illustration, page 194). For luncheon tables, pairs of figurines may take the place of candles.

Such designs are suitable for all three categories of arrangement mentioned in the first paragraph of this discussion, the only difference being that in Category 1 the composition must be constructed to be viewed from all sides and must be kept low.

Other possibilities are:

1. Water-lilies, camellias, gardenias, moonflowers, or hibiscus

blooms in a very low container, the flowers at varying heights and angles but very near the surface of the water. Self- or accessory foliage covers the needle-point holders and may extend horizontally over the edges of the container to give needed length. Never float flowers or foliage on the water itself but, by placing each stem in the holder, keep all blooms and leaves slightly above the water level.

Glass, silver, or ceramic water birds or fish, or figurines which seem to gaze into the water, often add interest.

The second category (2-A), where the floral arrangements are placed at the two ends of a long table, and (2-B), where one bouquet occupies the center of one side of a square or almost square table, usually close against a wall (see diagrams, page 166), is employed:

a. in order to use tall line material in table arrangements where guests are seated opposite each other (Diagram 2-A).

b. where the table is too long for the number of guests. They are seated opposite each other on the long sides, the ends being used for the arrangements (2-A).

c. where a refectory table is too narrow for an arrangement in the center but long enough for one at each end (2-A).

d. where guests are to be seated only on three sides of a table, the third side being against a wall (2-B).

e. where a small round or square table is set for three, the fourth place being occupied by the arrangement (2-C).

To execute a pair of arrangements for Diagram 2-A, make companion arrangements for each end of a long table. These may be identical or not, but if not, they should be related. As an example, a pair of low urns are used, in one of which is a line-mass arrangement of roses and snapdragons, with a bunch of grapes at the base. At the other end of the table, an identical urn holds bunches of the same variety of grapes, in a symmetrical composition, with a full-blown rose at the foot of the urn, the stem in a florist's tube of water which keeps it fresh and which is hidden by the foliage.

Arrangements for two ends of a table are most perfectly designed to be viewed from the guests' places at the table. The

Mrs. Fred W. Boschen, Jr. and Mrs. Harvey Traband, Jr.

Floral decorations for buffet tables are usually placed at the back rather than in the center, and should be non-tippable.

reverse sides, however, which are visible as members of the party take their places or walk from the table, are simply but attractively finished with fruit, flowers, or foliage, so that none of the mechanics of arrangement nor any bare, gaping holes are visible.

The same rule applies to arrangements for Diagram 2-C if the table is free standing, not against a wall, as it must be if the arrangement occupies space normally occupied by one seated guest. Any arrangement of correct size and proportion, coloring and design is allowable here.

For the arrangement at one side of a table which is against a wall, the back need not be finished. Here a larger and taller composition is permissible, especially if the wall is paneled or of a plain neutral color which will show to good advantage the silhouette of the arrangement. If a picture hangs on the wall, the arrangement may reach a corner of the frame but should not have any part of its design superimposed on the picture itself (see Diagram 2-B).

The buffet table (Diagram 3) gives the most latitude. Since there are no individual place settings, the floral composition (usually placed at the center rear) should be in scale, in height and length, with the size of the table and the food to be displayed. A very large buffet table may use a large arrangement, center rear, and two smaller ones at the ends, in which case the smaller compositions should be related in color and design to the large central one.

For a formal affair, urns, epergnes, silver or glass, stemmed fruit or cake dishes, rare vases of porcelain or glass may be used to hold the arrangement. Flanked by candles in branched sticks, candelabra, or hurricane lamps, and enhanced by decorative accessories in the spirit of the occasion, the buffet table for wedding, engagement, graduation, or coming-out party may be as elegant as one pleases.

On the other hand, the country breakfast before outdoor sport, the golf or tennis luncheon, harvest home or ski supper, or the habitual Sunday barbecue can feature containers suggestive of the occasion—flowers, fruits, and accessories which, combined, create rich still-life pictures of artistic merit.

The inspired hostess who enjoys "letting herself go," when it comes to floral decoration, should always serve her guests at a buffet table where possible, for here her genius can work untrammeled by limitations of place and space.

Tea tables for large social affairs habitually have an arrangement in the center of the table. If the table is free standing, the floral design must be viewed from all sides; if against a wall, from three sides only. Height is permissible here, if desirable, as the pourers at the two ends of the table will not be conversing with one another.

Still Lifes. The definition of still-life compositions in the National Council Handbook for Flower Shows is as follows:

". . . a grouping of plant materials (either fresh or otherwise) and other objects in which the story is told or the theme interpreted more by the objects used than by the choice and dominance of plant materials."

Mrs. Henry Hazen, Jr.

STILL LIFE of fruits and vegetables—the repetition of the general color scheme in the trailing bittersweet vine is a fine touch.

Mrs. Vincent Cronin

This all-green arrangement, with its Irish harp, shows what can be done by the imaginative artist for such holidays as St. Patrick's.

We cannot say that we are quite in accord with this interpretation, though the meaning is discernible. The Webster Dictionary definition of still life is:

"That kind of subject in a picture which consists of inanimate objects, as fruit, flowers, dead game, household utensils, etc.; also, a picture having this kind of subject."

We believe that a well-designed and executed still life need not necessarily tell a story or interpret a theme but that it should be judged on its beauty alone, unless a flower-show schedule specifically states that a still-life class is to be interpretive in character.

In our opinion, the careless yet ingenious beauty of a still-life painting by Cézanne, Fantin-Latour, or any of the other masters in this field, with rhythmic form, superb sense of design, and vibrant coloring, is something far above the studied, stylized perfection of a consciously conceived and meticulously executed still life interpreting Plenty, Poverty, Peace, or any of a score of other popular themes. To us it would seem that the ambitious arranger should strive to emulate the former rather than the latter type of still life.

In the strictly interpretive educational class where a beach scene, a forest glade, a bird sanctuary, or some other natural or man-made area is indicated, with the possibilities for its preservation or improvement, fine work is often done. Such classes are popular in the children's sections of many shows, and rightly so, for youngsters have a natural gift for this sort of thing. The Conservation Department often makes use of such classes, the children being asked to show the results of forest fires vs. fire protection, litter bugging vs. good outdoor housekeeping, and so on. Here is a constructive use of the garden club's interpretation of a still life, one which is educational and inspires the contestants to new efforts in a good cause. In the strictest sense, however, it is modelmaking.

Too often when adult flower-show schedules call for similar classes, the results are scarcely more mature than those of the

Esther C. Grayson

For a tray, use a low container with a large base so that there will be no danger of its upsetting en route.

juniors. One reason for this, we believe, is the fact that the creation of a well-balanced, well-designed model landscape is a difficult one, and one in which arrangers are comparatively inexperienced.

TRAY ARRANGEMENTS

Bouquets for the breakfast tray, the tea tray, or the invalid's tray should all be constructed so that they will be small enough not to overcrowd the limited available space, and so that they are very firmly balanced and not in danger of tipping over in transit.

A study of modern sculpture shows the unusual solidity of their bases, often achieved by heavy limbs when human figures are depicted. This characteristic of sculptural design is used to create that inevitable sense of balance which is needed in an arrangement for a tray. In order to assure this, comparatively low, chunky containers are indicated, containers either heavy in themselves or given added weight by being partially filled with sand or pebbles.

A single rosebud in a bud vase is suitable for a tray *except* that it is more than apt to upset in transit if the vase is of the usual tall, slim type, standing on a comparatively small base. A single rose for a tray, cut with a rather short stem and placed in a bottle or vase with a sturdy base and a slender neck, is beautiful, too, and is arranged in a container well suited for the use to which it will be put.

Small bouquets of mixed, short-stemmed flowers (including as many fragrant species as possible) in plump pitchers, or low globular vases with narrowed necks, have possibilities for use on trays, as have the real tussy mussies, arranged perhaps in a "hand" or antique five-fingered bottle container. In choosing the container, be sure it goes well with china or pottery being used on the tray. Fresh flowers may reproduce the floral pattern on the china, if any, in color, design, and actual plant material. An arrangement for a tray set with modern pottery in a plain, undecorated pattern is placed in a modern container. A few striking blooms with interesting foliage are arranged in a clean-cut, modern floral design.

Flowers which can readily be arranged for tray bouquets include:

Garden Material	*Florists' Material*
Blue lace-flower	
Calendula	
Candytuft	
Chrysanthemum (small)	Bouvardia
Cornflower	Carnation (bunch-flowered
Daffodils—miniatures	cluster type)
Forget-me-not	Camellia

Garden Material	*Florists' Material*
Fuchsia	Freesia
Geranium	Gardenia
Heliotrope	Marguerite
Lavender	Ranunculus
Lemon-verbena	Stephanotis
Lily-of-the-valley	Sweet peas
Marigold (dwarf)	Violet
Mignonette	
Nasturtium	
Pansy	
Pink	
Primula	
Pyrethrum	
Rose	
Rosemary	
Scabiosa	
Scilla	
Verbena	
Viola	
Violet	

MANTEL ARRANGEMENTS

A floral design for a mantel may be composed of two symmetrical arrangements; a pair of asymmetrical ones made to face each other to give a symmetrical over-all effect; a single symmetrical or asymmetrical composition in the center, flanked by candlesticks or other accessories; or an asymmetrical composition at one side balanced by an accessory or group of accessories of considerable weight at the other side.

Any such composition should suit the architectural features and period of the fireplace and mantel. A field-stone fireplace calls for sturdy, heavy, informal containers; marble suggests elegant containers and plant material. White carved colonial, dark polished wood paneling, or modern cut stone or slate are most enhanced by containers and compositions in a similar spirit.

If a painting or print hangs on the chimney face, the floral design flanks it and leads the eye toward it but never even partially obscures it. If a mirror hangs in the same position, an arrangement may be built up in back so that, when reflected in the mirror, it gives a dramatic illusion of depth.

Where the chimney face is undecorated, the floral decoration should be dominant and impressive, with strong vertical and/or horizontal lines reinforced by a massed center of interest to give weight and character.

If the mantel is high, a container of low or medium height, with plant material some of which droops in long sweeping lines, helps bring the composition down toward eye level. A tall vase of erect flowers on such a mantel makes it seem higher, and because it is so much above eye level, most of the design is lost.

Very low modern mantels, on the other hand, offer opportunities for the use of vertical designs or asymmetrical ones of considerable height and breadth.

Supplementary materials especially appropriate for use on mantels include Scotch broom, manipulated into the desired lines, ivies and other vines, procumbent artemisias; rambler and creeping roses, clematis, and the like.

MINIATURES

The miniature flower arrangement (the National Council's measurement for which is three inches over-all) appeals to the artist who likes fine detail and who is meticulous to a degree. Miniature arrangements, like miniature portraits, must be as perfect as the arranger can make them, exemplifying all the principles of good design, with special emphasis on *scale*. If one flower or leaf is too large for the other material or for the container, or if the vase is too large for the material, all illusion is lost. Those of you who have seen or have had an interest in creating puppet shows know that if every object and figure

Mrs. Wendell Kilmer

Miniature in close-up. Except for the dime in the corner that gives it scale, it might be taken for a full-sized arrangement. By blotting out the base of the pitcher with a finger tip it will be obvious that the container is a trifle tall for the height of the plant material.

At flower shows the class for miniature arrangements is sure to be popular with both exhibitors and the public. This "porthole" method of staging them (through openings cut in light plywood) has been used at the International Flower Show in New York. It not only saves space but displays the arrangements at eye level and is a boon to both judges and observers.

on the tiny stage is in scale the audience soon receives the illusion that it is viewing a full-sized stage.

An easy way of deciding on the correct size of each floral element is to remember that no single flower or leaf should be more than one third the size of the container, if perfect scale is to be maintained. After a miniature arrangement is completed, close observation under a magnifying glass will show up faults likely to be missed by the naked eye.

Techniques. The problem, then, in creating miniatures, is one of technique, since the art principles are the same as in any other design.

If containers with narrow necks are used, no holders are necessary. Opaque vases may be partially filled with sand in which the stems may be embedded. When glass or other transparent containers are selected, the underwater stems become part of the design just as in full-sized compositions.

For low containers, small lumps of florist's clay take the place of flower holders. Stems are embedded in the clay, and the holder is concealed by plant material.

Tools. A pair of cosmetic tweezers is best for placing material, as human fingers are too large to handle the tiny elements skillfully.

Mrs. Esther Wheeler

A miniature in which the scaling is just about perfect. The trumpet daffodil has been inserted to give an idea of its actual size.

Cuticle or very small embroidery scissors make a good substitute for the usual flower shears. With large clippers it is easy to prune away too much material.

For filling, emptying, and refilling miniature containers, use an eye dropper and remember that additional water will be needed every day.

Containers. In addition to the many miniature vases and other containers which are available in the shops, other objects may be utilized. Among these are small perfume bottles, tear bottles, lipstick cases, thimbles, pillboxes, and lids.

If a special shape or color is needed, a tiny container can easily be made of self-hardening clay, colored with oil paints, and the interior waterproofed with a coat of melted paraffin.

Bases can also be molded of clay and painted with black enamel.

Wooden ones can be turned on a small lathe, carved of soft wood, or sawed crosswise from a branch of required diameter, If desired, these can be stained, waxed, and polished.

Small, flat, water-washed stones, such as the large pebbles found on the outer beach here on Cape Cod, make interesting bases because of the variety of color and texture to be found among them.

If round forms are needed, the tops of rouge boxes or cosmetic-jar lids can be used "as is," or painted black; or if you are a photographer, your lens cap may be just the right size. The lids of small jewelry boxes, enameled black, make oblong bases.

Accessories. The arranger of miniatures can get much enjoyment from collecting not only containers but accessories. Tiny carved or ceramic figures and animals are often to be seen in the shops. Objects from daughter's small dollhouse may be useful. Very small sea shells, pebbles, seed pods, and berries can be incorporated in a miniature still life.

Plant Material. The selection of flowers and foliage for miniatures is an art in itself. Those who become deeply interested will constantly find new and beautiful growing things or will even grow them especially for the purpose. The following list is suggestive rather than inclusive.

ANNUALS
Ageratum
Arabis
Blue Lace-flower
Candytuft
Cynoglossum
Heliotrope
Linaria
Lobelia
Matthiola
Mignonette
Scabiosa
Statice
Sweet alyssum
Verbena

PERENNIALS
Achillea
Alyssum saxatile
Aubrietia
Cheiranthus
Dill
Eupatorium
Gypsophila
Heuchera
Lavender
Lantana

Myosotis
Nepeta mussini
Rosemary
Roses, baby
Thyme
Veronica
Viola
WILD FLOWERS
Arbutus
Bluets
Blue-eyed grass
Chickweed
Fringed polygala
Sand polygala
Scarlet pimpernel

BULBOUS
Chionodoxa
Daffodils
  (miniature)
Muscari
Scilla
Tritoma
HOUSE PLANTS
Acacia
Begonia
Bouvardia

Crown of thorns
Euonymus
Primula
  malacoides
Stephanotis

FOLIAGE
Baby tears
Clover
Grasses
Kenilworth ivy
Miniature ivies
Thyme

LINE
MATERIAL
Astilbe
Celosia
Gladiolus
  bulblet foliage
  Grasses
Lavender leaves
Rosemary leaves
Statice
  latifolia
Thyme sprigs
Twigs

Note: Use individual florets of multiple blooms such as alyssum, arabis, euonymus, and verbena.

DRIED ARRANGEMENTS

The art of making arrangements of dried material has grown and developed greatly since the publication of the first edition of our *Complete Book of Flower Arrangement* in 1947.

Artists with a keen sense of design have discovered many new opportunities in this specialized field.

For uncluttered modern interiors in private homes, clubs, meeting rooms, restaurants, and other spacious quarters where large, long-lasting floral decorations are desired, bold, clean-cut forms and lines are essential. These can be provided by driftwood, shrub branches, aspidistra, and ti leaves, combined with pods, cones, and berries to create compositions of sparse elegance. They are placed in heavy modern containers of good design, or antique bronze or copper urns, or vases of sufficient weight.

Flowers and foliage, carefully dried to preserve pastel tints of their original deeper hues, are used for many types of arrangement, large and small, both in the home and for exhibition work. These are delicate in both color and form, ideal for containers of Bristol glass, Parian ware, silver, pewter, tole ware, or fine porcelain.

Panels of bold dried material mounted on beautifully grained wood or fabric, and dried flower and foliage still lifes preserved in frames or in heavy glass paperweights have become increasingly popular as, displayed in this way, they are permanently preserved. Panels reminiscent of the exquisite bas-relief garlands and wreaths of the Classical and Neoclassical periods are among the eminently successful aspects of the art as practiced today. These feature dried leaves, pods, cones, and berries in variety, arranged with formal symmetry (see page 289).

Dried compositions suggesting the seashore, displayed either on baseboards or mounted on wood panels, offer endless possibilities. Driftwood, shells, cork floats, corals, sea fans, starfish, sea horses, sand dollars, dried seaweeds, beach grasses, and other dried beach growths provide a rich harvest of materials.

One of the most ingenious modern uses of dried material is that of combining it with semipermanent plants like coniferous and broad-leaved evergreen branches, and with fresh cut flowers. In such an arrangement the main line, or skeleton is constructed of driftwood, dried vines, embryo palm hearts, bayberry, dock heads, or other dried line material permanently anchored in a container. To these are added secondary elements of evergreen foliage and focal interest of fresh, colorful flowers, which are replaced as needed. One of my most cherished designs consists of dried material in a wooden mortar. Embryo palm hearts form an *S* curve with supplementary lines of wheat, dock, yucca pods, sea-grape leaves, sweet-gum pods, and deodar "roses." For special occasions, pieris leaf clusters are quickly and easily substituted for the sea-grape, and crimson carnations or florists' anemones take the place of the yucca pods as a focal feature.

(For drying techniques and lists of plants suitable for drying, see Chapter 22.)

14

ARRANGEMENTS
FOR SPECIAL OCCASIONS

Arrangements for the great holidays of the year, family anniversaries, and individual celebrations present special problems even as they offer unusual opportunities for original and creative work.

To make compositions in the spirit of an occasion, which yet uphold the best traditions of good taste and design, is a real challenge to the artist. It is much too easy to place a fat china infant in the center of a dish of paper white narcissi on New Year's Day; or going to the other extreme, to construct something so obscurely symbolic that it must be explained to the guests in order that it be understood and appreciated.

Naturally, one must also be guided, to a certain extent at least, by those for whose enjoyment the occasion is being planned. But here again, good taste is of as much importance as good design. The fact that a group of guests may be accustomed to candy cherries and paper hatchets on the George Washington Day table is no excuse for continuing the custom. A clever and well-designed adaptation, however, would probably be received with more enthusiasm than something so completely new and different as to make it difficult for guests to identify it as symbolizing the birth of the father of our country.

Whatever the composition and whatever the occasion, appropriate accessories lend style and interest. Just as candles, stars, and angels give authority to Christmas decorations, so there are symbols for the other holidays. It is the function of the arranger and home decorator to incorporate these in her work in such a way that they will be in good taste, never blatant or overemphatic but used as an integral part of the design, well correlated to the chosen color scheme.

Long gone are the days of red paper or candy hearts for Valentine's Day or of red, white, and blue paper streamers for the Fourth of July. Now the arranger uses her own imagination and ingenuity to tie in her chosen flowers and accessories with the special occasion being celebrated.

THE NEW YEAR. New Year's Eve and New Year's Day, as two of the most joyous occasions on the calendar, should have floral decorations which are gay, brilliant, and sparkling.

A composition for a New Year's Eve buffet table may feature swinging silver bells which really ring when agitated. These, with snow-sprinkled or completely frosted evergreen boughs, ring in the New Year from buffet or hall table. A bottle of champagne on a silver tray wreathed with frosted ivy or smilax may be surrounded by beautiful crystal saucer glasses, in each of which is placed a gardenia corsage or a jasmine boutonniere as favors for the guests.

For New Year's Day, masks of comedy and tragedy are tossed with apparent casualness on a tray of exotic fruits—pomegranates, hothouse grapes, and Du Comice pears.

Or place an open engagement book for the New Year, with a quill pen and antique silver or brass inkstand, beside a vase or urn of massed, mixed flowers to represent each of the four seasons: for spring, the blooms of hardy bulbs; for summer, roses, stocks, snapdragons, or delphinium; for autumn, chrysanthemums and asters; and for winter, evergreens, carnations, and freesias. If the flowers for each of the four seasons can be segregated into individual groupings which blend gracefully with each other, the composition will present the desired effect.

All February holidays, strangely enough, traditionally call for red as their dominant color—and at a season when few red flowers are available.

LINCOLN'S BIRTHDAY, which comes first, suggests simple pioneer containers and accessories, such as an oaken well bucket on a base made of a rough wooden slab or "shake," in which red geraniums are arranged. As accessories, use a slate and pencil or a candle in a primitive holder burning beside an old, hand-printed, calfbound textbook.

If something more formal is needed, an old print or a bust of Lincoln may be placed on a chenille table cover, or a man's shoulder shawl of the period, with a Victorian vase or even a stovepipe hat massed with dark red carnations, roses, and snapdragons.

WASHINGTON'S BIRTHDAY requires quite different treatment. Here a "Williamsburg" arrangement in any traditional container of the period may be employed with such accessories as a sword and hat of a Revolutionary Army officer, a surveyor's sextant, a bust of Washington, or a facsimile of the Declaration of Independence.

For a modern arrangement to suggest the day, use bare cherry branches for line material, glossy foliage such as that of gardenia or camellia, and cranberries wired in to simulate bunches of cherries. As a container, use a tall narrow, cylindrical cherry log with the bark on, polished or varnished to preserve its finish and hollowed out to hold an invisible metal or glass water container.

ST. VALENTINE'S DAY, being a sentimental occasion, may be celebrated at a table where a Dresden cupid aims his deadly darts toward a bisque maiden hiding behind a vase of red sweetheart roses or lilies-of-the-valley arranged with a bunch of sweet violets bearing a red rose at its heart. An ornate container of French china, decorated with flowers and gold leaf, is appropriate to the spirit of the day.

Those who collect figurines will find many groups or individual figures of the Rococo period in France well suited to use on St. Valentine's Day. Shepherds and shepherdesses, a beplumed beau with his demure fair lady; a young girl in bisque net ruffles—these are a few examples.

Today, if one desires, the center of the table may form a gold and lace paper valentine with a central motif in which a heart-shaped china or silver dish is closely packed with the heads of red roses or carnations.

For a children's party, arrange a lace-frilled old-fashioned bouquet destined for each guest, in a heart-shaped design on a red silk velvet heart in the table's center, with a red ribbon leading to each place card.

A glass and silver epergne, with its many tiers and side bowls for small nosegays, is an eminently appropriate container for a St. Valentine's Day table, and this may be used for the most formal of adult settings. Red should dominate if mixed flowers are employed, and dark, blood-red (not Christmas red) candles in silver candelabra or branched sticks.

ST. PATRICK'S DAY, like the February holidays, is one which has long been distinguished for the ugly and unimaginative decorations often used in celebrating it. Yet few special days offer such rich possibilities for originality. After all, the hostess can use the traditional color without blinding the guests' eyes with a mass of emerald green. When I was a child, coconut creams rolled in cinnamon were sold in March to simulate Irish potatoes, but luckily these seem to have passed into the same relative oblivion occupied by licorice shoestrings.

An antique Irish harp, or a gilded replica, or one simulated of spring flowers, with vine strings, makes an appropriate central motif.

Of course there are endless combinations of all-green plant material in addition to the tiny-leaved shamrock. An interesting design can be created using several shades of green, from the greenish off-white of some varieties of caladium leaves to the deep greens of calla and strelitzia foliage. Because of the time of year, northerners, at least, will have to depend on the florist or on house-plant foliage for living green. Oxalis, with its handsome trifoliate leaves, is showier than shamrock yet suggests it. The arranger might also try Bells of Ireland, if in the market, or dried sprays which can be tinted a delicate green and gold if they have lost their natural color. A Waterford glass goblet or pitcher makes a good container.

A table decoration for laughs is an open handmade basket, or an inverted billycock hat, filled with scrubbed small Irish potatoes and surrounded by a wreath of real shamrock in concealed pots or of oxalis foliage or miniature ivy. A shillelagh, bound with greens or spring flowers, is laid beside the basket or hat.

EASTER offers all sorts of arrangement possibilities, the preferred colors being white, lavender, and pale yellow.

Because Easter lilies and Calla-lilies are the flowers most often used for this occasion, it seems less trite to find other suitable plant material unless the arrangements are to be used as church decorations or as altar flowers. Materials which suggest themselves are blue, white, and yellow bulbous iris; anemones and tulips in the same color range; white trumpet, triandrous and larged-cupped lemon and white daffodils; violets, freesias; stocks; spathiphyllum and eucharis. Mimosa also lends a touch of yellow.

As Easter represents to many of us the coming of spring, this phase of the holiday can be emphasized in table and living-room arrangements. (It's religious connotations seem rather too solemn for treatment in decorative motifs.) White candles make accessories which are suggestive of aspiration without the use of angels or religious figures. Arrangements also should be up-reaching, the tips of all plant material pointing upward.

An Easter table for a children's party may combine a low basket of green- and yellow-dyed Easter eggs with a loose bouquet of field violets and the fiddleheads of young fern fronds. Or a china setting-hen dish can be filled with dyed or chocolate coconut eggs, wreathed with a garland of mixed spring flowers, rather like the circlets which sometimes appear on leghorn hats.

MAY DAY has now fallen into disrepute as a Communist holiday, but in New England, at least, it is still remembered and celebrated as the spring festival.

A May Day party should, of course, feature the May baskets which young people once filled with flowers and food delicacies and hung on the doors of friends. (In the part of Connecticut where one of us grew up, the ritual prescribed that the recipient of the basket was to chase the giver—who usually managed to get caught in the end—and bring him back to the

house to partake of the contents of the basket and other refreshments.) The girl who received the most May baskets automatically became the most popular. An amusing variation of
this custom at a young people's party would be to arrange a
flower-decorated basket of refreshments for each couple, each
boy to select his choice and then choose a girl with whom to
share it.

MEMORIAL DAY arrangements for the home should certainly feature peonies and iris, which are then at their height.
In arranging peonies for a buffet or side table, take a leaf from
Oriental flower art. A full bloom, a half-open blossom, and a
bud with self-foliage in a wide, shallow container give twice
the satisfaction to be derived from a heavy bouquet of the huge
blooms. The same is true of iris, especially of the Siberians,
though bearded varieties may also be arranged with three or
five long stems and with buds, half-open, and full-blown flowers in a low dish in the Moribana style.

For a patriotic Memorial Day meeting or service, a wreath of
bronzy beech, leucothoe catesbaei, or laurel leaves may sur-
round an iron helmet filled with red Oriental poppies.

June is the month of graduations, brides, and roses. A wealth
of other garden material is also available at this time: Madonna
lilies, Oriental poppies, the blooms of laurel, rhododendron,
syringa, and spirea, in addition to the orange blossoms and
orchids of the florist.

WEDDINGS. White flowers in glass, silver, or marble, with
accessories such as ceramic doves or a small marble replica of the
famous Cupid and Psyche group, are suitable for the bride's
table. Intertwined, narrow wreaths of golden yellow flowers,
suggesting a double-ring ceremony, may be placed flat on the
cloth, with a vase of flowers rising from each to create a single
composition. One of these should be taller and more massive to
suggest the masculine, the other light, airy, and feminine.

The arranger can really go to town when it comes to the
bridesmaids' and ushers' table, for here the color scheme may
be planned to blend with that of the girls' costumes. Tablecloth,

glass, and china, as well as flowers and accessories, may be chosen with this color scheme in mind. Pairs of figurines, and rather large ones, will add much to the gay brilliance of such a table. Some of the modern dancing figures in rhythmic poses are beautiful enough to suggest the floral design to be used.

Mrs. Louise Hoffman

Arrangements for special occasions always add a note of gaiety and festivity, especially if they are so designed as to be particularly appropriate to the event, such as roses in silver for a silver-wedding anniversary.

WEDDING ANNIVERSARIES come in June, too, of course, and these, featuring the material (silver, glass, gold, and so on) of the particular celebration, should be as elegant and elaborate as the wedding table itself. For the twenty-fifth, or silver anniversary, silver containers and well-arranged red roses make a hard-to-beat combination. The golden wedding usually features yellow flowers as well as gold-decorated china, glass, and flower containers. Stems of Bells of Ireland, lightly sprayed with gold paint, will give beautiful flowing curves for line material to be combined with yellow roses, rich metallic rex begonia foliage, gold-variegated house plant foliage, or golden-leaved forms of privet, arbor-vitae, or locust.

A GRADUATION PARTY may feature a table arrangement in which simulated rolled diplomas are used for height. Placed vertically and close together at varying heights, these give the effect of several lengths of bamboo often used in Japanese arrangements. A "mortar board" used as the base for the arrangement is another amusing possibility.

For any of these June celebrations, an old-fashioned bouquet may be simulated as a central decoration for the table. A large, round, very shallow glass dish is filled with appropriate plant material: for example, the heads of small roses, garden carnations, delphinium, and balsam florets, arranged in circles as in an old-fashioned bouquet. Around the edge place a wide frill of real lace, and at one side, well tucked under the edge of the container, a large, loosely tied ribbon bow with many loops and streamers.

FOURTH OF JULY, coming in the heat of the summer, is likely to be celebrated outdoors at the barbecue grille or the swimming pool, and consequently decorations are pretty informal.

A red-and-white checked and fringed linen tablecloth for the outdoor table gives two of the essential colors. In its center a Revolutionary powder horn filled with bachelor's buttons may be supported by a small drum with a fife lying across it, or even by a blunderbuss or other weapon of the period.

Our two autumn holidays, Halloween and Thanksgiving,

Esther C. Grayson

This tray of autumn fruits and nuts, with a hunting horn used as a horn of plenty, is given height by the bamboo vase filled with late flowers. The rough-hewn tray blends in texture with the bamboo, as do the candles with their spiral pattern. Candleholders are of hand-carved, natural wood.

have the same general color scheme of turning leaves and harvest richness.

HALLOWEEN is largely for the youngsters and consequently too much subtlety probably will not be appreciated. An arrangement featuring a pair of black ceramic cats, highly glazed, gazing into a black glass dish heaped with candied apples on sticks, is a welcome change from cutout witches and pumpkin heads. For a long refreshment table where a troop of scouts or a school class is to be seated for an evening party, a series of lighted pumpkin heads down its center, graduated in size from large to small, may be placed on a base of red oak leaves, with Indian corn ears and husks to give variety.

For an adult party, use a gnarled branch of driftwood for an eerie line composition on which may be hung character masks. Deep orange calendulas make a good choice for plant material in such a composition. If placed on a console table, a round, undecorated brass tray placed against the wall behind the arrangement gives the effect of a huge, rising moon.

THANKSGIVING arrangements, whether casual or elegant, should, it seems to us, reflect the bounty of the harvest season. Consequently, we prefer mass or line-mass arrangements which convey this feeling of plenty more emphatically than those which emphasize line alone.

Fruits and flowers and/or vegetables and nuts may be ingeniously arranged in a split complementary, triad or tetrad color harmony, heaped on a base, tray, or in a handmade basket or horn of plenty (see illustrations, pages 136 and 194).

Height is provided by using richly colored autumn flowers and foliage, vertically arranged and blended into the over-all design. A slim wine bottle may be used as an accessory to give height. Ceramic or silver pheasants, cocks, turkeys, and ducks also make effective accessories. Large birds should be reserved for the "sideboard" or buffet as they are somewhat too realistic for the dinner table, but smaller ceramics and replicas in glass or silver are acceptable. Fine period figurines in Pilgrim costumes also are good. For a horizontal line to finish off a low, massed arrangement on a long table, use a sweeping, curved line of bright red cranberries, sprays of berried juniper, or broad-leaved evergreen branches accented with stalks of dried wheat or oats and small nuts.

Glass hurricane lamps, half-filled with crimson cranberries and holding lighted red candles, make a colorful and timely pair of table accessories for an evening meal.

In general, we advise the use of edible harvest fruits rather than gourds, Osage oranges, ochra, and pine cones. While beautiful in themselves these are less suitable for Thanksgiving than for other occasions.

Other possible accessories for informal tables include decoys; antique copper or wooden molds and utensils such as cran-

Mrs. Anne Elizabeth Erhorn

The brimming abundance of the autumnal season is well conveyed in this colorful composition for a harvest festival. Exotic material, allowable in a flower show, would, for a home decoration, be better replaced by locally available fruits and/or vegetables.

berry pickers, scoops, scales, and measures (most of which can be used as containers).

For greater formality, use a traditional marble or bronze urn, a large epergne, or tall stemmed glass or silver fruit dish, massed with a combination of flowers and fruits. A white marble urn heaped with crimson pomegranates and spilling hot-house grapes can have all the classic beauty of a carved frieze.

Christmas greetings

An antique fruit dish is correctly arranged with all the reckless abandon of a still-life painting of flowers and fruits by one of the old masters. Bronze urns suggest classic restraint, with large central fruit or vegetable forms and symmetrical bunches of grapes overflowing the sides. In making such an arrangement, keep in mind the rich but classic simplicity of a Roman mosaic or Greek fruit sculpture.

CHRISTMAS, *the* holiday of the year, has its traditional decorations which are preferred by those of us who are "old-fashioned." Little need be said of these except to suggest that wreaths, swatches, and other decorations of greens, berries, cones, and so on can and should be well designed, even if traditional in spirit. *Artificial holly berries and glossy, weather-proof plastic ribbon bows can spoil any decoration.*

Our own preference is for present-day interpretations of the traditional, but employing living greens and berries.

Wreaths of cones, seed pods, and nuts in their natural colors, or touched here and there with gold or with artificial snow, can be used year after year if they are well made, each unit being firmly wired to the foundation so that the design is sturdy and permanent. Each Christmas season these may be mounted on somewhat larger, flat-topped wreaths of fresh greens such as hemlock, pine, balsam, or box.

The same is true of Della Robbia wreaths of shellacked fruits, nuts, and pods, though either may be used without a base of fresh greens if desired.

Recently there has been a growing preference for gold and green, or white and green, instead of the traditional green and red.

Mantel decorations, table arrangements, and *door swatches* or *wreaths* are designed of fresh greens with accents and focal interest of pods, nuts, berries, and cones trimmed to suggest flowers, sprayed with gold or white paint. Milkweed and unicorn plant pods, dried ochra, bayberry, magnolia leaves and fruits, and dried Bells of Ireland are other preferred materials for spraying. In some arrangements, the whole is sprayed with white artificial snow.

If a silver spray is desired, aluminum paint, which is sold as silver, gives an unpleasant, harsh metallic effect. In experimenting over the years, I have found that the addition of a little gilt paint takes the curse off and gives a delicate silver-gilt color which is charming. In fact, I seldom use either gold or silver alone but mix the two as desired, more gold than silver for a gilt effect, and just a touch of gold in the aluminum paint for a gilt-tinged silver.

Then, too, I always use the spray bottle with restraint so that portions of the natural browns of the pods and the pale greens or silvery whites of milkweed and Bells of Ireland remain visible. The result is less overpowering but more subtly effective.

The *Christmas garland, or festoon,* much used today, is of ancient origin. In our mother's day, a very inartistic phase of this type of decoration was the looping or twining of yards of laurel ropes or precious ground pine.

Around pillars and over doorways and mantels. Today, the arranger forms a mantel or doorway garland in the old classic tradition. Backed by coniferous or broad-leaved evergreens, the surface is built up with cones and pods, nuts, berries, shellacked fruits, or what you choose. As a pattern, study examples of the carved garlands which were so prominent a feature of interior architectural decoration in Rome in the first century B.C. and again during the Classic Revival in Georgian England. A wreath of the same materials is a good choice for door or chimney face.

Wall trees are clever space savers for small rooms or can even be used as door decorations. Build a symmetrical tree-shaped background of branches of short-needled evergreen or box and trim it with the amusing European ornaments once again available—birds, bells, musical instruments, flying angels, and so on—or with edibles such as lollipops, candy canes and clear candy animals, Christmas cookies and string bags of nuts. If a formal effect is desired, arrange the decorations in a studied, symmetrical design suggestive of a Byzantine spire arrangement (see Chapter 11).

Mobiles. For sophisticated interiors, large Christmas mobiles are often more appropriate than the conventional tree. If hung in a slight draft, to produce constant motion, the glittering balls and other decorations are a constant pleasure to the eye.

Instead of using wire clothes hangers as most amateurs do, select a long, gnarled and branched piece of blueberry or manzanita. This may be rubbed to a soft, natural glow, sprayed with white enamel, or even painted with cold-water paint. Suspend this from the ceiling by a thin, all but invisible copper wire, and then, mounted on a sturdy ladder, place the decorations at various levels to create perfect balance when completed.

Modern trees. Another decoration very similar in effect is made by spraying a gnarled and twisted bare branch with white, mounting it in plaster of Paris, and decorating it with Christmas ornaments. For several years we had fun making these, which our friends called the Rockwells' Death Valley Christmas trees.

Table arrangements combining greens (or greens frosted with mica "snow") and Christmas-tree balls, or balls alone on a mirror base, are easy to make, yet gay and colorful.

Red fruits, such as apples, grapes, cranberries, and pomegranates, may be combined with poinsettias, red roses or carnations, holly, and other Christmas greens, for the dining table or buffet.

For a large table, compositions may include flowers, greens, Christmas candles, Christmas bells, and/or figurines in any preferred color harmony.

In living rooms and halls, combine English holly, with its glossy dark green or variegated leaves, and other greens with berries or red fruits. Here, too, is an opportunity to use the green and gold, green and silver, blue and white, or pure white arrangements discussed earlier in this section.

15

ARRANGEMENTS TO WEAR

During recent years, arrangers have become interested in using fresh flowers and foliage to make their own corsages, bouquets, garlands, bracelets, and decorations for the hair.

This is a very natural development of floral art, as by practicing it, the skilled artist can create individual personal adornments to fit her personality, to enhance her costumes, and to point up special occasions of all sorts.

So popular has this phase of arrangement become that many clubs have engaged professionals to instruct them in the mechanics of corsage-making so that their work may be crisp, long-lasting, and in every way equal (or superior) to that of the florists.

By using flowers and foliage fresh from the garden or window garden, the arranger attains the special satisfaction of displaying on her person material which she has herself grown —and at a fraction of the cost of "store-bought" corsages. Many women like to make their own corsages even during the winter when they must buy the plant material. By doing so, they are able to wear, for a very modest outlay, ornaments of distinction and originality.

HOW TO DO IT

Any living plant material to be used for corsages must be well hardened overnight, or for at least six hours, in deep water, in a dark, cool place.

Florists' supplies, which can be purchased from a wholesale supply house or from a local florist if he is good-natured and accommodating, are:

Florists' wire, Nos. 22, 24, and 27

Floral tape or parafilm, in green and brown

Chenille-covered wires (like pipe cleaners) in green, brown, and white

Florists' ribbon in several colors

Corsage pins

Scotch tape

Wire cutters, floral shears, sharp knife, scissors

The two most important techniques in corsage making are *wiring* and *taping*.

Double flowers like carnations, marigolds, and roses should have their stems removed just below the flowerhead itself. A wire is run through the calyx of the flower, then doubled and twisted to the length needed for the artificial stem. The floral tape is now applied, starting it high up on the wire and firming it well with the fingers. The stem is then twirled between thumb and forefinger to bring the tape up above the

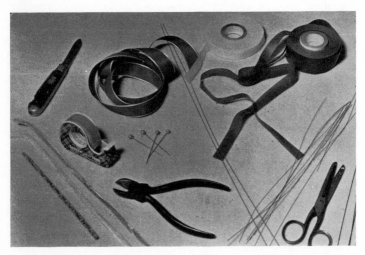

1. Equipment and supplies

2. Severed rose being wired

wire and around the lower part of the calyx, then down again,
still twirling, but in reverse, to the lower end of the wire (see
illustrations). The tape is held in the left hand, and the stem
twirled with the other, to produce a tight, neat twist of tape
around the double wire. In the case of smaller flowers, instead
of using a double wire for the artificial stem, it may be twisted
together just below the flower head and one end snipped off,
leaving a single wire to be taped.

3. Foliage (grape-ivy) is added

4. Corsages—commercial and homemade

Supplementary foliage may now be added. In illustration 3, a grape-ivy leaf is being added to a rosebud as it is more long-lasting than rose foliage. Attached to the flower stem with wire, it is then taped to the rose stem. Three such leaves are enough for an average rose corsage of perhaps five blossoms.

In illustration 4, a homemade rose corsage with grape-ivy leaves and roses facing in two directions is contrasted with the average uninteresting, inexpensive florist's corsage with asparagus fern and a bow of ribbon.

5. Method of wiring flowers with shallow calyx—such as blue lace-flower

6. *Single wire is pushed up through calyx, then bent into hook and pulled back.*

Flowers which have shallow calyxes, such as blue lace-flower, scabiosa, marguerites, and so on are wired in a different manner. The stem is cut to one or two inches and a wire pushed up from below through the head of the flower. Now a very small hook is formed at the top of the wire, which is then *pulled back* until it is hidden in the heart of the flower. The wire "stem" is then taped as before.

There are two main reasons for wiring and taping. First, it prevents the possibility of wilted stems which would cause the whole corsage to collapse. Second, the wires make it possi-

7. *Bracelet of roses, with matching velvet ribbon*

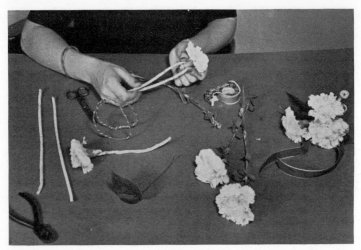

8. *Making a bracelet; foundation is formed of three wires taped together, bent to fit wrist.*

ble to bend and face the flower heads in any desired direction.

In making an old-fashioned, formal bouquet, the flower heads are removed and each is wired *but not taped*. When all are assembled in the desired design, the stems are taped as a unit. Paper frill and ribbon bow are then added. Galax or ivy leaves can be substituted for the lace paper if desired.

To make the wristlet shown in illustration 7, study the technique in picture 8. Three No. 22 wires are cut long enough to

9. *Proof of the pudding—various types of corsages*

go twice round the wrist. These are taped together and bent back to make a double circle, open at one end. The taped wire is then covered with a suitable ribbon, which is twirled on over the tape and fastened at each end with Scotch tape. The bracelet should now be fitted to the wrist. Flowers are wired and taped as for a corsage and firmly secured to the center of the wristlet. If chenille-covered wire is used for the flower stems (as in illustration 8), the ends can be rolled around a pencil after the stems are fastened on. These make attractive "tendrils" and can be used with or without an additional ribbon or velvet bow (as in illustration 7).

10. Floral shoulder strap, neckpiece, and comb

In photograph 9, six simple but effective homemade corsages are shown, each one quite easy to make. Beginning at the top left, we have red carnations with foliage of *Cissus antarctica* (from the winter window garden); gladiolus florets and buds, with rhododendron leaves; marguerites, pansies, and sweet peas surrounded by cissus foliage and tied with ribbon. Below (left to right): pompom chrysanthemums with pale green ribbon; violets and marguerites surrounded by galax leaves; an old-fashioned bouquet of pompom chrysanthemums and dwarf double marigolds, edged by cissus leaves and tied with a perky bow.

In illustration 10, a floral shoulder strap combines carnations and wide velvet ribbon; a neck ribbon decorated with a tiny bouquet of sweetheart roses; and a comb for the hair on which have been wired pompom chrysanthemums and ivy foliage. The imaginative arranger will plan all sorts of floral decorations of this sort. Cocktail "hats" of fresh flowers are often worn, as are wreaths of fresh flowers, to match evening costumes. One perfect rosebud with a bit of foliage, perfectly wired and taped, makes a charming decoration for an evening bag. There are endless possibilities.

Until the novice learns how to make corsages and other decorations for personal adornment, she can practice with garden flowers, odds and ends of ribbon, ivy foliage, and other readily available material. Once she has the "hang of it" she need not be afraid to wire and tape her most beautiful blooms.

CORSAGE MATERIAL FROM THE GARDEN AND WINDOW GARDEN

FLOWERS

Annual:

Arctotis
Bachelor's buttons
Balsam
Bells of Ireland
Blue lace-flower
Browallia
Candytuft
Marigold
China aster
Cynoglossum
Gerbera
Godetia
Heliotrope
Lantana
Mignonette
Ornithogalum

Pansy
Petunia
Salpiglossis
Scabiosa
Schizanthus
Snapdragon
Stock
Star of Texas
Sweet pea
Tahoka Daisy
Torenia
Wallflower
Zinnia

Perennial:

Achillea
Campanula

Chrysanthemum
Coral bell
Delphinium florets
Dianthus
Feverfew
Forget-me-not
Gypsophila
Lavender
Primulas
Pyrethrum
Roses
Shasta Daisy
Violas and violets

Bulbous, hardy:

Daffodils
Fritillaria

Hyacinth
Lily-of-the-valley
Muscari
Lilies
Scilla

tender:

Anthurium
Freesia
Gladiolus
    florets
Gloriosa-lily
Orchid
Ornithogalum
Stephanotis

Vines:
Shrubs;

Azalea
Camellia
Clematis
Lilac
Gardenia
Philadelphus
Pussy Willow
Viburnum

FOLIAGE

Annual:

Begonia
Coleus
Columbine
Geranium
Sedum
Vinca rosea

Perennial:
Shrubs,
Vines:

Camellia
Clematis

Coral bell
Elaeagnus
Galax
Ginger
Ivies
Hollies
Pachysandra
Passiflora
Pieris
Pittosporum
Primula
Rosemary
Smilax
Vinca minor

House Plant:

Camellia
Cissus
Geranium
Gardenia
Ivies
Vinca major

Part Four

THE PRACTICAL SIDE

Esther C. Grayson

GARDEN FLOWERS for home decoration—lilacs for spring; annuals for autumn. These are ten-minute decorations, just for pleasure.

16

SELECTION AND HANDLING OF PLANT MATERIALS

To remain crisply fresh as long as possible, flowers and foliage must be cut at the right stage of development, at the right time of day, and must receive correct care and handling. Most of us, at one time or another, have seen a recently perfect, long-stemmed rose hang its head and wilt completely within an hour or two after cutting. Occasionally an inexperienced exhibitor loses a blue ribbon because a specimen bloom or a portion of the material in an arrangement fails to hold up long enough for the judges to see it in perfect condition.

It pays, therefore, to learn at what stage to cut material, at what time, and how to handle it to insure the maximum life span.

When to Cut. The cool of the evening is the best time to cut, especially in hot weather. After the sun has been down long enough for garden plants to recover from the hot afternoon hours, take a pail of room-temperature water with you to the beds where you wish to cut. Recent experiments have proved that less shock is sustained by cut material if it is placed in water not too much colder than the surrounding air. As the cool of night arrives, the water cools gradually.

As you cut each stem for the following day's arrangements, place it in the pail or pails, being careful not to overcrowd the receptacles in such a way that stems may become entangled. If this is the case, leaves or even flowers may be torn off when they are removed. We prefer to use plastic pails with rolled edges. These are light to carry and less likely to injure blooms and foliage than is a metal bucket.

Early morning is the next best time to cut, and is, indeed, an ideal time if the weather is cool. At this time of day the plants have profited by the coolness and humidity of a long, dewy night. Then, too, there is seldom very much wind in the early hours of morning.

Wind is an enemy to cut flowers. In very breezy weather, place the pails in a sheltered spot against a building, fence, or wall or in the lee of shrubbery.

What to Cut. Here is a guide for cutting flowers at the right stage of development to assure longest life:

ANNUALS: as soon as they are open or two-thirds open. Avoid day-old blooms

BULBOUS FLOWERS: half-open if possible. Otherwise just opened.

CAMELLIA: freshly opened

CHRYSANTHEMUM: freshly opened cluster flowered: open, half-open, and buds

DAHLIA: two-thirds open

DAY-LILY: in bud, showing color

FRUIT TREES, FLOWERING: in bud, showing color

GARDENIA: in bud, or just opening

IRIS: in bud, half-opened, and just open

PEONY: in bud, showing color to one-third open

PERENNIALS: freshly opened

POPPY: in bud, showing color

ROSE: to keep: in bud, after calyx has turned back and a few petals have unfurled; to use next day; one-quarter to one-half open, depending on variety. Singles open quickly; doubles, slowly

SPIKE FLOWERS (*Delphinium, Larkspur, Lily-of-the-valley, Lupine, Montbretia, Snapdragon, Stock*): lower florets freshly opened; upper florets in bud

WATER-LILY: when *first* opened

Aftercare. From the garden, bring the cut material to the flower room or kitchen.

Spread newspapers on counter space and remove material from pails, one stem at a time, being careful not to bruise or tear blooms or foliage. As each stem is removed, strip foliage to above water level in finished arrangement. Remove thorns from roses or other thorny stems.

Recut stems on an angle. For flowers that wilt easily, hold stems *under water* in pail in which they are to harden overnight, and recut. Do not remove stems from water after recutting until you are ready to arrange flowers.

Prehardening treatment for woody stems. Chrysanthemums, buddleia, and other woody stemmed perennials; shrubs, tree branches, and evergreen boughs should be split vertically at the butt with a sharp knife. Make two or three of these slits to facilitate water absorption.

Before hardening bulbous flowers, wrap the bottom inch of each stem with soft string or raffia to keep from curling back. This is especially necessary with daffodils.

Flowers which bend while hardening, like calla-lilies and tulips, are rolled for their entire lengths, including the blooms, in several thicknesses of newspaper before placing them in pails to harden.

Special treatment for difficult flowers. Before hardening, sear stem ends in a gas or candle flame and then place in deep water at 80 degrees to harden:

Artemisia	Hollyhock
Campanula	Lantana
Chrysanthemum	Oleander
Euphorbia	Platycodon
Geum	Poinsettia
Heliotrope	

Place stem ends in *boiling* water (do not let steam reach blooms) and then harden in *cold* water:

Daffodils (harden in 3 to 4 inches water only)	
Dahlia	Hydrangea
Forget-me-not	Poppy
Fuchsia	Stephanotis

To harden, place these in warm water, 80 degrees, but *do not sear:*

Beech	Mockorange
Calceolaria	Nasturtium
Calendula	Nicotiana
Cineraria	Paulownia
Crape-myrtle	Primula
Evergreen branches	Salvia
Laurel	Snapdragon
Lavender	Sweet pea
Heather	Tithonia
Mertensia	Verbena
Mignonette	

Submerge completely in cold water for a half hour before regular hardening:

Christmas-rose	Flowering shrubs in bud
Lenten-rose	Hydrangea
Flowering fruits in bud	Lily-of-the-valley

Place stems in *three to four* inches of water to harden:

Anthurium	Lily-of-the-valley
Cyclamen	Lotus
Freesia	Pansy
Gerbera	Sweet pea
Iris	Water-lily

OTHER TREATMENTS

Glycerin and charcoal: Wash in soapy water. Rinse and dry. Split butt ends. Spray branches with clear plastic. Add one teaspoon glycerin and several small lumps charcoal to each quart of water in container. Use this in arrangement. Change weekly.

Beech branches	Oak leaves
Evergreen boughs	(Soak in ½ glycerin, ½ water overnight to preserve autumn color. Then arrange in above mixture.)

Boric acid: (To retard bacterial growth and decay.) Add ⅛ teaspoon boric acid to each quart water when hardening. Can be used for any plant material.

Salt: Add 1 tablespoon salt to each quart water for hardening.

Achillea	Hollyhock
Bamboo	Marigold
Begonia	Plume-poppy
Coreopsis	Tuberose

Sugar: Add 1 tablespoon sugar to each quart of water for hardening.

Aster, China	Nigella
Aster, hardy	Petunia
Chrysanthemum	Sweet pea
Daisy	Verbena
Gaillardia	

Vinegar and sugar: (To acidify alkaline water.) Add 1 teaspoon vinegar, 1 teaspoon sugar, to each quart of water for hardening.

Azalea	Laurel
Cattail	Rhododendron
(Also spray heads with clear plastic to keep intact.)	

Wax or plastic: Coat reverse side of leaf or berried shrubs, with transparent wax (plant glaze) or clear plastic to reduce water loss.

Caladium	Berried shrubs:
	Hollies
	Junipers
	Pyracantha

Drop a few drops warm paraffin in heart of flower at base of petals to hold blooms open.

Passion-flower	Water-lily

Hardening. After recutting, defoliating, and giving other desired special treatments, place the material in water at room temperature (or warmer if so stipulated in special instructions) and store in a cool, dark place, such as a cellar or dark, dirt- or concrete-floored garden house overnight, or for a *minimum* of six hours. Except for the few species which do better in shallow water (see above), fill the pails to within an inch of the tops.

Keep out of direct drafts during hardening period.

Commercial cut-flower preservatives (such as Floralife or Bloomlife) may be added to the water in which material is hardened if no other special treatment (the use of glycerin, sugar, salt, and so on) has been resorted to.

Exceptions. The following flowers are *not* placed in water to harden in the usual way, but are treated as follows:

Pack in moist newspaper after spraying with *fine* mist of water. Do *not* place stems in water.

Acacia	Galax
Ferns	Violet

Pack in tight box in refrigerator, covered with moist cotton. Do *not* place stems in water.

Bouvardia	Gardenia
Camellia	Tuberous Begonia

Orchids only. Split stems vertically for one inch at base. Insert stems in orchid tubes of cool water. Refrigerate in tight box. Remove stems from tubes for one hour each day to prevent saturation of petals.

Warning: Waterdrops on the petals will spot

Camellias	Sweet peas
Lilies	Tuberous begonias

Lilies should also have the pollen-bearing anthers removed to prevent the pollen from staining the petals.

17

CONTAINERS, BASES, ACCESSORIES, AND BACKGROUNDS

CONTAINERS

The definition for "container" in the National Council of Federated Garden Clubs' *Book for Flower Shows* is: "Any receptacle for cut plant material." We have been unable to find, in the present edition, any reference to the base on which such a receptacle may stand, but we know that such bases are considered integral parts of arrangements in judging. That is to say, an arrangement of fresh plant material in a container, standing on a base, qualifies as a flower arrangement. The base is not considered an accessory.

Given a basketful of flowers freshly cut from the garden, or a florist's box of hothouse blooms, what are you prepared to do with them? Do you have a container of the size, shape, and coloring to enhance the floral design you make of this plant material—one which fits well into the décor of your home?

If you can say "yes" to these questions, you already have at least the nucleus of a container collection suitable to your individual needs. If the answer is "no," the chances are your bouquets of cut flowers seldom do justice to the plant material of which they are composed.

Garden Club members who enter arrangement classes in flower shows soon learn the importance of containers in that fascinating and highly competitive sport of striving for blue ribbons and other awards.

Often a well-chosen, out-of-the-ordinary accessory can "make" the arrangement or even inspire it. Here a perfectly selected ceramic crane not only becomes an integral part of the design but by repetition of form and color adds a real punch.

Esther C. Grayson

Basic containers. These shapes, in neutral colors, will prove useful with many types of flowers and for a variety of floral designs.

Again and again at flower shows we have seen the coveted awards go to arrangements in which the container—or more accurately, the suitability of the container in relation to the plant material and its design—was the deciding factor in determining the prize.

Perhaps you are not at present interested in flower-show competition, but even if you use cut flowers only to decorate your home, you need a number of containers.

BASIC CONTAINERS

In selecting these, the first consideration must be given to *shape*, and the second to *color*. *Texture* and *quality* are also of importance.

Containers which are of tall and medium height will be needed, as well as broad, shallow dishes or bowls. In order to take care of all types of plant material, these will have to be available in several sizes.

For purposes of discussion we have selected from our shelves a group of basic shapes, shown in the illustration on page 221. These and others similar to them are the ones we use most frequently, especially for simple, quickly-made everyday decorations for the house.

The tall, *tubular* vase at the extreme left is of Oriental inspiration, where containers of natural bamboo originated, although the one shown is of softly glazed, cream-white porcelain, American made. This basic form may vary in height, diameter, and in the material of which it is made. Japanese tubular containers often have side openings in which to place supplementary plant material at various levels. We use this shape, which we have in several sizes, colors, and textures, for tall flowers like gladiolus, delphiniums, chrysanthemums, and flowering shrub branches. The straight sides make it easy to secure stems in place. A holder or a few inches of sand in the bottom, or a forked stick inside the mouth, is all that is needed. Tall vases which flare at the top or even those which curve inward, above rounded shoulders, tend to let stems and branches swing outward at "unknown angles."

The *brick*, or *pillow* vase in the upper center of the illustration is an ancient shape which has proved generally useful through the centuries. It is available in many sizes, materials, and colors. Heavy glass and glazed pottery are often used. The opening is sometimes at the top, as in the vase illustrated, sometimes on the side, which produces a container wider than it is tall. This basic shape is sturdy because its broad base helps give balance to even quite heavy material. We use pillow vases for annuals such as marigolds and zinnias, and for geraniums, small dahlias, and China asters. With these round forms, for line material we add *Salvia farinacea*, snapdragons, larkspur, artemisia, Chinese delphiniums, *Nepeta Mussini*, or eupatorium.

The necked vase at the upper right is a form of the classic vase used throughout the world from the remote past to the present. The length and thickness of the neck and the exact curves of the vase itself vary greatly in individual specimens,

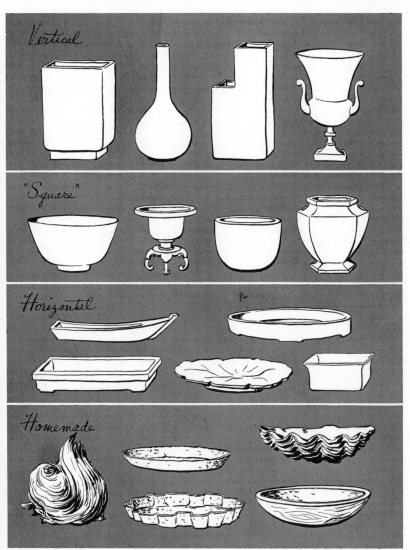

Collection of containers

but all have small bases with a swelling bowl above, drawn in to a narrow neck, straight or flared, often with a decided lip.

These vases are well suited to symmetrical mass arrangements if not too heavy, as well as for asymmetrical line-mass designs.

The urn (see illustrations, pages 221 and 223) is closely related to the necked vase.

The bowl, or round dish (lower left) is of moderate size, depth, and weight. A hand-made pottery piece, the pale decorative motif is too indeterminate to draw the eyes to it from the flowers it contains. Bowls vary in shape from the globe (usually of glass), with a small opening, through the half sphere, to very shallow, circular dishes. Sometimes the tops flare out as in Revere silver bowls, which are supported on bases. Sometimes the upper edge is simply sheared off as in a chopping bowl. Again, the opening is drawn in somewhat as in the example in the illustration. They are available in all sizes. The arranger should be supplied with a number, or with modifications.

The oval bowl, or straight-sided shallow dish is one of these. (See illustrations, page 221 and 223.)

The *oblong dish* at the lower right is a basic Japanese form, and one which the arranger will find indispensable. In this example there are rudimentary feet, and the dish itself is somewhat bowed, its long side walls being slightly curved upward. We have an American-made dish of approximately the same design, but slightly wider and without the bow. More than once I have removed a partly constructed arrangement from this and started over in the Japanese dish. In some subtle way its design is perfect for asymmetrical line arrangements and for Moribana compositions.

A modification of this shape is a deeper, oblong, straight-sided dish, also of Oriental inspiration. This also often has rudimentary feet, and the sides are gently flared, sometimes straight but often with a curved upper lip. (See illustrations, pages 221 and 223.) These are most often available in pottery, porcelain, or bronze. They are ideal for asymmetrical line-mass arrange-

Mrs. Henry Swaebe

Selecting the container often has much to do with the success of the arrangement. The old pewter pitcher and plate are just right for the nasturtiums (above), while the vase and figurines (below) exactly suit the exotic character of the plant material—ginger blossoms and croton leaves—in an arrangement "Reminiscent of the Philippines."

Mrs. Dunham C. Jones

ments emphasizing line, the massed center of interest being close to the water surface.

Other Practical Shapes. Each arranger has her favorite containers and usually she prefers certain forms that particularly suit her styles of composition.

The following are well worth serious consideration:

The *vase, bottle,* or *flagon* with a rounded body and neck much longer and more slender than in the necked vase discussed above. These may be of glass, pottery, or porcelain.

The *tall jar with rounded shoulders* (see illustration, page 221). A modification of the straight tubular form, this shape is excellent for heavy branches and very large material, such as sprays of lilac, long-stemmed tulips, iris, and the like.

The *bean pot, ginger jar,* and *stoneware pickle jar* are modifications of this shape.

For those who enjoy making line arrangements in the tradition of the classical or orthodox Japanese schools, a genuine bronze *usubata* (see illustration, page 223) is a "must." Not unlike a classic urn with handles, but standing on three curved feet, it holds heavy branches without fear of tipping, while the wide, shallow, removable dishlike top can be used or not as the arrangement requires.

Distinctive Containers

In addition to basic shapes, most arrangers wish to own a few very distinctive containers just as a well-dressed woman's wardrobe will include a ball gown and an evening wrap.

If the collector has plenty of money to spend, she buys, wisely or foolishly, according to her taste. The better containers in our collection—of marble, Swedish glass, Bristolware, bronze, and so on—are all of neutral colors because we must make our outlay give the best possible value, just as the purchase of an expensive dress is based on its wearability for many different occasions.

For us poor mortals, there is a way to make a well-shaped container serve often. It can be temporarily colored or tinted for use in a specific arrangement. Tintex, water colors, or tempera may be used, and, having served their purpose, removed.

For those who can afford it, many treasures are available —hand-made pottery vases which are in themselves rare works of art; Swedish, Finnish, Corning, and Venetian glass vases;

Esther C. Grayson

Containers for roses should be of fine glass, porcelain, or metal. This Aurene bowl of deep, iridescent blue makes an ideal foil for yellow roses.

Oriental and European dishes, urns, and vases of fine porcelain or rich metal; rare goblets, flagons, and mugs; epergnes and fruit dishes.

Containers of natural wood or stone. Collecting driftwood, cypress knees, laurel burls, and other wooden pieces to convert into naturalistic containers is a hobby indulged in by many arrangers, and one which can yield rich rewards. For dried arrangements these can be used without a water container but for compositions which include living plant material, a metal or glass container must be concealed within or behind the wooden object.

Soft sandstone, soapstone, and similar soft rock can be drilled and hollowed to make interesting primitive containers. If not impervious to water, the interior is made so by coating it with melted paraffin. By concealing a dish, bottle, or other container for water behind lumps of rose quartz, glass slag, and similar materials, the clever arranger can often get just the shape and color effect she wants.

Converting other objects. Some ingenious women haunt second-hand shops and even dumps, bent on finding discarded articles to convert into containers. The decorative tops of old Franklin and potbellied parlor stoves; metal lamp holders; china, glass, and metal oil-lamp bases; antique scales; wooden measures, scoops, dough bowls, mortars, and cranberry pickers; metal or carved wooden chests and boxes; baskets of all sorts; antique copper, tin, or ceramic utensils such as molds, candle molds, spice cans and cases; pottery and stoneware jars, pitchers, and pots; shells and lengths of ceramic tile are among the objects often utilized.

Make Your Own. An interesting hobby for the arranger who is a craftsman is the study of ceramics in order that she may make her own pottery containers.

BASES

Though a base is considered an integral part of any arrangement in judging artistic classes in a flower show, the subject of bases must be considered as a separate one.

Often they are important elements in floral design. A formal Japanese arrangement in a bronze *usubata* would be unfinished without the teakwood base on which it stands, just as less formal compositions are usually placed on bases of natural or polished wood cut crosswise or at an oblique angle from a log and measuring one or two inches in thickness. Similar bases cut from heavy burls are even more beautiful. Taborets and bamboo mats and rafts are also much used.

Sets of polished black wooden bases, oblong, round, or oval in shape and graduated in size, should be in every arranger's collection. Several can be used, one on top of another, as a base for one vase when it is necessary to give added height.

A set of three polished, black composition bases of free asymmetrical forms in assorted sizes is a favorite of ours. Round, oval, and oblong bases of marble, slate, and polished stone and clear or colored mirror bases with beveled edges often fit well into compositions.

For informal arrangements, inverted trays of wood, basketry, or metal and mats of bamboo, reeds, grass, or fiber are often appropriate. Bricks, blocks, or flat water-washed stones are other possibilities.

Elegant containers demand bases of similar quality and fineness of finish, and the opposite is also true. Rough-textured heavy vases and dishes are enhanced by sturdy, dull- or rough-surfaced bases.

ACCESSORIES

Until recently, dried materials, driftwood, and anything whatever except fresh plant material were defined as accessories by the National Federation of Garden Clubs. A newly adopted directive of the National Council, however, has changed all this so that a container with the material used in it to create a floral design is now correctly designated as an arrangement.

Accessories are the objects, not *in the container itself,* which may be used to complete or enhance the design or to suggest a theme.

The creative arranger makes use of the most unlikely objects to complement her compositions.

Small sculptures, carvings, figures of bird, beast, and *Homo sapiens,* including very ancient objets d'art and those which

RIGHT

WRONG

RIGHT

WRONG

RIGHT

WRONG

Plan each arrangement to fit its assigned location. Design, scale, balance, harmony must all be considered. Which principle has been violated in each "wrong?"

are modern; useful objects such as bells, inkstands, pens, clocks, hourglasses, comfit and snuff boxes, fans, lanterns, candlesticks, paperweights, books, jewelry, minerals, semiprecious stones, rocks, pebbles, bricks, or shells are but a few commonly used accessories.

To employ these effectively, however, one must have the sense of artistry which can compose a unified design of container, plant materials, and accessories, a design which is harmonious in spirit as well as in color, texture, form, and scale.

Scale indeed is most important in the use of accessories. A figurine too large or too small for the proportions of the arrangement itself can easily destroy the beauty of the whole design.

BACKGROUNDS

In many flower-show classes the exhibitor may, if she chooses, provide a fabric background or drapery. In the home, also, a special background can greatly enhance the over-all effect of an arrangement. A background, then, is the "surface against which things are seen or upon which things are made or placed," according to the definition in *The Book for Flower Shows*.

Choosing such a background is a tricky business and calls for good judgment and restraint. How often we have seen entries in shows in which the arranger's choice of a background disturbed the unity of a composition instead of adding to it!

In the first place, arrangements appear to maximum advantage against unpatterned surfaces. Therefore, even the most charming and highly appropriate figured wallpaper, fabric, or screen may draw attention away from the floral design, no matter how well suited it may be to the theme of the composition.

Where there is pattern without mixed colors in a background material, it can sometimes be used to advantage. Examples are lace shawls or veils; embroidered or woven fabrics where de-

BACKGROUND: Here figured backgound makes it impossible to take in clearly the design of the arrangement, and accessories add to the confusion. Use of plain screen background and removal of accessories clear up the composition. The dark base gives design the stability it formerly lacked.

sign and material are of the same color; or figured wallpapers in shades, tints, or tones of a single color.

If you disagree with this general statement, have a color photograph taken of an arrangement or composition in which a multicolored fabric or other background has been used and compare it with another, taken against a neutral one. Years ago at one of the big spring shows, all backgrounds in niches included simulated black wrought-iron grilles. No photographs taken that year did justice to the arrangements, and in many cases the arrangements themselves were spoiled or made less effective.

18

MECHANICS OF ARRANGING

A comfortable place in which to make arrangements is most helpful. So much equipment is needed that flower rooms are being built into many modern homes, with adequate waterproof counter space, cupboards, shelves, running water, and a slate or linoleum floor impervious to water damage.

Most of us, however, cannot afford a flower room. If a substitute must be planned, the best available spot in most cases is the laundry room. A set of extra cupboards and shelves for containers and equipment are usually all that need be added, as laundry rooms today usually have counter space. In old houses, the butler's pantry makes an ideal flower-arrangement room.

I myself arrange in the kitchen, for my new modern kitchen has enough cupboard space for containers and other equipment, plenty of formica counter space, and a stone floor.

EQUIPMENT

Each arranger has her favorite equipment. The items starred are essential to success. Many others are optional.

2 to 4 plastic buckets with rolled edges and bail handles
   1 large, light pitcher which pours well
* 1 small, light watering can with long spout
* A collection of containers, tall, medium, and low, large and small. Almost every home has enough to start with. Add a few each year

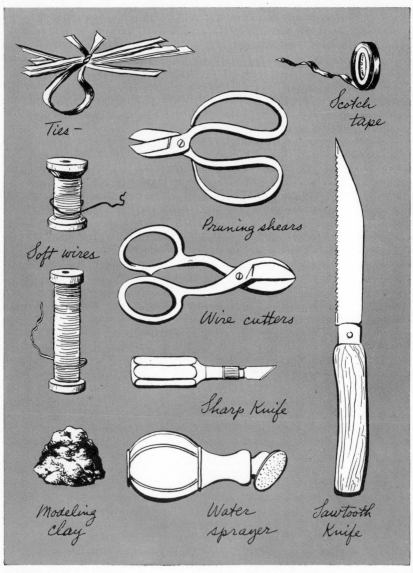

Ties –

Scotch tape

Pruning shears

Soft wires

Wire cutters

Sharp Knife

Modeling clay

Water sprayer

Sawtooth Knife

For a good job of arrangement, secure the right tools and equipment.

* A collection of bases, round, oval, and oblong
* 1 pair large pruning shears
* 1 pair small pruning shears
  1 pair cutters which grip stem of flower
* 1 sharp knife
* 1 bundle or spool fine wire
* 1 bundle or spool medium
  1 roll corsage tape, green
  1 roll corsage tape, brown
  1 roll corsage tape, white
* 1 spool corsage thread
  1 bundle long pipe cleaners
  1 bundle short pipe cleaners
  1 package long Twistems
  1 package short Twistems
* Floral clay, waterproof, non-hardening
Floral clay for dried arrangements
* Pin-point holders, the more the better, in assorted sizes
  Chicken wire, cut in 6-inch squares
  Sand (to fill tall vases)
  Vermiculite to fill vases
* Hammer for crushing woody stems
* Toothpicks or wired floral picks
* Chopsticks, or lengths of smooth woody twigs, for lengthening stems
  Orchid and florists' tubes
  Chewing gum
  Rubber cement

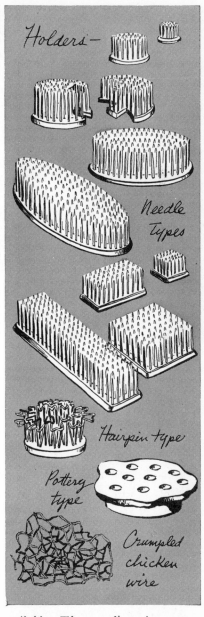

Holders—
Needle Types
Hairpin type
Pottery type
Crumpled chicken wire

Holders of many types are available. The needle-point type, which comes in many sizes and shapes, is the most useful.

CONSTRUCTING AN ARRANGEMENT: Shown above are the steps usually followed in putting together an arrangement. First comes the selection of materials and container; next, the blooms, sprays, or foliage that will determine the main line are placed; then the center of interest (focal point) is added; and finally, the "filling in" is completed. The color scheme should be

In adding to your collection of containers, you can spend a fortune in time or money or both. Many arrangers make some of their own, either of ceramics or metal, or by converting common useful objects for this use. Oblong or pillow-shaped wax cans, wine or liquor bottles, lengths of ceramic tile pipe, and sheets of plumber's lead may be converted into containers by changing the color and finish, cutting to the desired height, bending into the needed form.

When buying containers, it is well to remember that most flower designs look best in undecorated vases of neutral colors which do not draw attention from the flowers themselves.

determined in advance. One color (which may include several of its tints, shades, and tones) should dominate. In the arrangement above, blue was selected as the dominant color. The flowers are in tints and tones of violet-blue, with a touch of orange as a complementary contrast.
Arrangement by Mrs. Esther Wheeler and Mrs. Charles G. Scholz

Period arrangements are exceptions to this rule as these must be placed in vases or urns of the period, many of which were ornately decorated. If you can afford a considerable investment, a few handsome hand-made ceramic containers of fine form; one or two of Swedish or Corning glass; a few authentic Oriental containers of bronze, pottery, or bamboo; a marble urn of classic design; a silver bowl; several modern metal containers of copper, bronze, or pewter will provide your basic needs.

Bases should include round, oval, and oblong teakwood stands of Oriental design or inspiration. Any wood painted black, rubbed down, and waxed will provide a satisfactory finish. Bamboo rafts of various sizes are also most useful. Bases of beautiful wood, cross-cut from burls or large boles, rubbed, waxed, and polished, can be made at home if the budget is limited. Round and oval shallow fish and kipper cans, unopened, painted black, rubbed down, and waxed, are excellent for bottles and bottle-shaped vases. Straw or split bamboo table mats; round and square ceramic tiles; pieces of slate, waxed and polished; wooden butter-pail lids; metal can and pail lids, enameled and waxed, are among the "make-it-yourself" bases which can be very satisfactory. Bases of any desired shape, including irregular, modern outlines, may be made of plaster of Paris poured into a box lid, pan, or other form. When hard, remove from mold, tint, paint, shellac, or otherwise finish as desired.

Accessories may be many or few, ranging from priceless figurines and miniature animals to fans, boxes, jewels, lumps of glass slag, rocks, pebbles, birds' nests, and the like. The more you have to choose from, the better. Those who have been wise enough to keep antique miniature figures and other "what-not" treasures will find them most useful. The important thing to remember is to use an accessory only when it is in scale and in the spirit of the arrangement. Any accessory, of course, should enhance rather than detract from the composition as a whole.

HOW TO DO IT

The skill with which you use your equipment is most important. I should know for I am by nature "slapdash." I am always in a hurry and hate to take the time to do it right. Every time I take a short cut in arrangement construction, however, I regret it.

Securing Pin Holders. Most arrangements today are secured with pin holders, except for those in tall vases. Unless the pin holder is tightly affixed to the bottom of the container, the arrangement may tip over or shift position.

Be sure the containers and pin holders are *perfectly dry*.

In a metal container, secure the holder by pouring paraffin under and around the holder until it is firmly set. (Floral clay tarnishes silver and pewter.)

In a ceramic container, roll between the hands a piece of floral clay until you have formed a long, thin roll or "worm." Place this around the entire edge of the holder and press down on the bottom of the container until it adheres firmly. In containers too deep or too narrow to admit the hand, press holder down on bottom with stout sticks or woody stems if any are to be used in the design. Be sure the holder is *firmly set*.

Placing Material in Pin Holders. The placement of heavy material often poses a problem. Large chunks of floral clay worked around the base of the stem or branch and into the holder usually do the trick. Heavy flower stems may often be driven on the pins at an angle opposite the one desired. The stem is then pulled over to the correct angle and a lump of clay, or a second stem, is wedged against it to hold both firmly. Holders are never permitted to show in a finished arrangement. Cover with foliage, pebbles, flat stones, glass chips, or moss, always selecting material harmonious with the spirit of the arrangement.

To remain efficient, the pin points of the holders must be kept erect and in place. If some are bent by a heavy branch, straighten them out with an old-fashioned watch or clock key, or with a little gadget sold in arrangers' shops especially for this purpose.

In using glass or plastic containers, select pin holders small enough to be completely covered. Make underwater stems and leaves *a part of the design*. Place stems, and if necessary accessory foliage, on pin holder so that it is entirely covered. Attach floral clay "worm" to edge of holder. Place in *dry* vase. When you are sure the design is satisfactory, *but not before*, press firmly to attach to bottom. Then add water.

For line-mass effects, first fasten a pin holder to the bottom of a *dry* container. Next place line material, securing the stems in the pin holder. Then stuff the open portion with cut evergreens or florists' ferns, shearing the stuffing off just above the mouth of the container. Set stems of mass design in this stuffing.

Fillers for Vases. There are many methods of arranging in tall containers and in those of considerable depth but with wide openings. These can be partially filled with sand so that the stems stand upright when sunk to the bottom.

Lighter and easier to handle, however, is a stuffing of arborvitae, juniper twigs, or florists' fern fronds as mentioned above. These are placed in the vase in an upright position, stuffing it quite full. Then the tops are sheared off a little above the opening.

Other Methods. Some artists prefer crushed chicken wire stuffed into a container, or uncrushed wire stretched across its mouth, to the evergreen stuffing. I have never found either very satisfactory.

Heavy iron tubular holders, made in the Orient, can be used for arranging bulbous flowers with thick round stems in low dishes, but each tubular opening must be snugly packed with stems to hold the flowers upright.

If pin holders are used for bulbous flowers, bind the base of each stem with florists' thread to keep it from splitting and curling up. It is to prevent this that the Chinese and Japanese cut an entire clump of daffodils, leaves and flowers, retaining the outer covering which keeps the stems from splitting.

Florists' thread is also valuable for binding into clusters small blossoms or mixed groupings which are to be used as units in an arrangement.

Thus, in a table arrangement which must be finished on two sides, one placement of line material is visible from all angles, but two similar groupings for central interest (one to be viewed from each side) can be arranged in the hand, bound with thread, and slipped into place in front and in back of the one taller line design. Groups which are to be placed in profile, or in reverse, at the sides or toward the back of a larger arrangement, to give three-dimensional depth, are more easily managed if first bound with thread to make easily manipulated units.

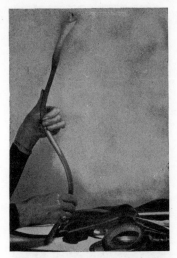

CONSTRUCTING THE ARRANGEMENT: Stems. *Above, left: Calla as cut. Right: bending stem by gentle, repeated pressure to obtain just the line wanted. Flowers and foliage are then grouped in the hand and tied, to save time in assembling arrangement at show. At right: completed arrangement in place. Leaves under water hide stems; lighting simulates sunshine; glass brick base is harmonious.*

Demonstration by Mrs. Anne Elizabeth Erhorn

FOLIAGE. Large leaves can be made to stand upright or assume desired curves by using florist's wire, held in place by Scotch tape on the reverse side. Below: finished arrangement— wired foliage held erect instead of flopping; wings on figure carefully painted to pick up color of anthuriums.

Demonstration by Mrs. Anne Elizabeth Erhorn

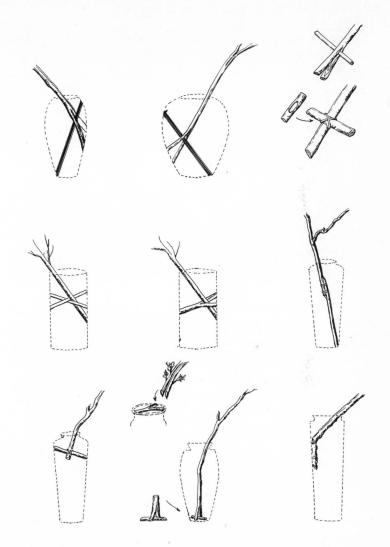

The Japanese have developed their own methods of holding flower stems at desired angles. To master those illustrated, all that is needed is a little experience and skill.

To make leaves, especially large ones, retain desired curves or angles, tape pieces of wire *on the backs*, along the midribs, using Scotch or masking tape. They can then be turned in any direction. This works especially well with such leaves as dracaena, calla, anthurium, strelitzia, monstera, and so on.

Pipe cleaners are useful in coaxing accessory foliage, such as large-leaved begonias, to droop over the edge of the container at just the right angle to cover the stuffing and tie in with the other material. The cleaners can be used as accessory stems which will bend in any needed direction.

For fragile straplike leaves, such as those of narcissus, day-lilies, or Siberian iris, place several in a group and wire each group at least one third its length so they will stand upright when placed in a container. The wiring, of course, must be adequately covered from the eye of the observer.

For line arrangements in tall jars or straight-sided vases of bamboo or ceramic—the Najiere, or leaning designs of the Japanese, for example, where only a few stems are used—a forked stick, or crossed sticks bound together at the crossing, may be forced inside the opening of the vase below the water level. If a single shrub branch is used in a vase, the stem can be forced into the cleft of a partially split stick placed snugly across the container below eye level.

Some artists prefer to hold heavy stems with strips of plumbers' lead twisted around the stems and caught over the side of the jar. This works well only with straight-sided containers, and the lead must be covered with other plant material.

How to Secure Fruits and Vegetables. For arranging trays, baskets, or compotes of fruits and/or vegetables, with or without flowers, fasten small pin holders to the bottom of the container where you wish to place some of the fruits. If flowers are to be used, fasten a low container in the desired position, with pin holders for fruit surrounding it. Make the flower arrangement. Then impale on the pin holders several of the largest fruits or vegetables, always keeping your design in mind. Fasten each remaining fruit or vegetable to a wired florist's

Flowers and foliage for main
lines are cut or bent to the desired curves and secured in a
heavy holder placed in the
container.

Shorter stemmed flowers are
used to complete the curve;
and a center of interest is added
by one large or several small
blooms.

Small flowers and foliage are
used to fill in and to break horizontal line of container—but be
careful you do not overdo this.

The completed arrangement,
placed on a stand that is in
scale (in size) and in harmony
(in color and texture) with it.

pick and place each by driving the picks into the fruits impaled on the pin holders. If needed, finish off with small fillers, such as nuts, cranberries, or sprigs of evergreens, in the interstices.

A FEW TIPS ON CONSTRUCTION

1. For vertical *line-mass designs*, whether symmetrical or asymmetrical, place the tip of the main line of your design directly above the spot where base of the stem enters the pin holder. Height should be roughly one and a half to twice the height of a tall vase, or the *width* of a wide shallow dish.

Next add supplementary line material, two thirds to one third the height of the first line, to establish the outline, or skeleton.

Now place short-stemmed material for accent and focal interest.

2. In making *horizontal designs*, first place the three main lines, establishing the height, which will be about one third the diameter of a wide container. Next determine the horizontal extent, which can be roughly one and a half to twice the diameter.

Add shorter supplementary material, following the first three lines.

Add emphatic forms for central interest and accent.

3. If a *curved, circular,* or *crescent-shaped design* is being constructed:

Establish main curves.

Add shorter, supplementary material, following main lines.

Place short-stemmed, larger flowers near center for focal interest.

4. For a *symmetrical* mass design:

Place central line, rising from the exact center to a point one and a half to twice the height of the container.

Now place two sides lines, one on each side of center, establishing outline of arrangement.

Insert filler material to make a solid, symmetrical mass design.

Place focal forms, low and near the center, balancing symmetrically on each side of center. One large form, or a group of smaller ones used as a unit, may be placed near the rim of the container exactly over the axis.

19

ARRANGEMENTS IN COMPETITION

The arranger who, for the first time, plans to enter competitive classes in a flower show faces a new challenge and a whole set of new problems. Instead of making arrangements entirely to suit herself, as she does when decorating the rooms of her own home, the flower-show exhibitor must follow the prescribed schedule and rules to the letter if an award is to be won. (See sample schedule, page 259, and sample rules, page 260.)

If your club is not affiliated with your state Federation of Garden Clubs or with The Garden Club of America, but is an individual, independent organization, it can make its own rules and regulations for flower-show practice and staging. In general, however, these will follow the pattern of procedure set up by the National Council of State Garden Clubs, Inc., the national organization of the Federation. *The Handbook of Flower Shows*, published by the National Council, gives specific instructions on staging, exhibiting, and judging, as well as on what constitutes an "arrangement" and a "composition." If your club belongs to the Federation, the show committee will draw up its schedule and rules in conformance with the advice offered in this book, so it is advised that each exhibitor thoroughly familiarize herself with it.

Take, for example, Class 2, Section I in the sample schedule on page 259, calling for "a composition in a silver, pewter or glass container, roses predominating; to be staged in a niche

32 inches high, 28 inches wide, 18 inches deep, 40 inches from the floor."

The size of the niche stipulated in the schedule will automatically determine the over-all dimensions of any arrangement displayed in it, for it must fit into that space without touching any of the boundaries. In this case, therefore, its dimensions cannot exceed 31 inches in height, 27 in width, and 15 to 17 in depth, and should be considerably less.

An inexperienced arranger entering this class, faced with the problem of only two or three perfect roses ready for picking at the time of the show, may think "Oh, well, I'll just fill in with other flowers." But unless roses *predominate*, the judges cannot award a prize in this class, no matter how excellent the design. A line arrangement, using the few available roses and just a little other material, would, however, conform to the schedule and give the entry a chance to win.

The container for this entry must be of silver, pewter, or glass, and nothing else will do, even though it may be your most cherished rose bowl. The "glass" category, however, is a wide one, in case you do not wish to use metal. Unless you are prepared to make the underwater stems an integral part of the design, it is better not to select clear glass. Opaque containers, such as those of Venetian glass, do not pose this problem.

As for accessories, you may use them or not in a class where accessories are "permitted," not "required." In Class 2, Section I, accessories would be a necessity since the class calls for a composition. These accessories may consist of figurines or other objects of weathered wood or dried material (see definition above) if your club is adhering to federation requirements.

In addition to all this, the plant material must be crisp and fresh, the arrangement of an excellence that will permit the judges to give it a winning score.

Since the title of the class is "Last Roses," it might be well to use as supplementary material with the dominant roses something typical of autumn, such as a berried shrub or foliage

Mrs. Otho E. Lane

The effective distribution of dark and light values in this design gives it stability and distinction. The heavy base and sturdy jar provide an adequate base for the massed flowers and graceful shrub branches.

which has taken on its fall coloring, for in an *interpretive* class the composition should suggest the thought behind its title.

TYPICAL CLASSES

Themes. Where a theme is chosen for the arrangement section of a flower show, as in the sample schedule, "Time of

Harvest" (page 259), each class is planned to interpret some phase of that theme, and the contestant who would win a prize should give much thought to this.

In Class 3, for instance, "Bird Harvest," a St. Francis figure and accessory bird figurines would be the obvious interpretation. Something more original but equally interpretive might have a better chance of winning.

Niches and Shadow Boxes. Classes to be exhibited in separate niches or boxes are the most challenging, since the perfection with which they are displayed and lighted calls for equal beauty of color, design, and structure. In these classes, clean-cut lines and well-placed masses are a necessity. Any carelessness in execution is immediately apparent. The rank amateur might better begin with an arrangement staged in a smaller space, on a table or shelf.

HOW TO WIN BLUE RIBBONS

The winning of awards for flower arrangement is a career in itself. The satisfactions to be gained from it are the pleasures of artistic creation, the stimulation of striving in keen competition, and the accumulation of assorted ribbons, plaques, vases, and other trophies of victory.

Such a collection of awards may also lead to more substantial returns, for today there are scores of competent arrangers who earn comfortable small incomes from articles and lectures and from doing arrangements professionally for social affairs, hotel lobbies, store displays, and the like. The first step toward any of these remunerative activities is the winning of blue ribbons in amateur competition. Of course, however, the real professional can no longer compete in amateur shows.

How should one set about winning blue ribbons?

The first step, if the matter is to be taken up seriously, is to get as thorough a knowledge as possible of the general principles of flower arrangement. There are dozens of books on

Mrs. George Goldson   *F. F. Rockwell*

DECORATIVE: An arrangement that does not require the expression or interpretation of any particular idea or theme, but aims merely at beauty, as in this deceptively simple but exquisite combination of sunflower heads and plume-poppy foliage. EXPRESSIVE (Interpretive): An arrangement (or a composition) that serves to express or interpret an idea or theme, for instance, the somewhat bizarre but amusing Midsummer Happiness.

special phases of the art. A list of many of these is to be found in the Addenda at the close of this volume.

The next step is to attend a flower-arrangement school. These are now carried on by leading garden clubs throughout the country. In addition to these, there are also the post-graduate or judges' courses. Private classes are often organized and a teacher of good reputation engaged by a group interested in the subject.

However, we did not set out to write this chapter for the career woman in flower arrangement. By the time she reaches that stage, she is well aware of all possible ways of improving her techniques.

Let us, then, get back to the beginner who, with some

Mrs. Stuart DuBreuil   *Mrs. George Goldson*

ARRANGEMENT: This artist has used only fresh plant material, container, and base. The metallic sheen on the rex begonia foliage and silvery black baptisia seed pods repeat the satiny patina of a container made by the exhibitor.

COMPOSITION: This beautifully conceived and executed composition on the Jungle Rhythm theme is by the same artist who arranged the driftwood and dried sunflowers in the arrangement on page 252. Here, figurines, fungi, embryo palm hearts, and other dried materials are combined with the ginger blossoms, palm fronds, and croton leaves to create a three-dimensional composition of real distinction.

trepidation, had decided to make a first attempt at her local flower show, by entering the lists in a jousting match with her fellow arrangers.

STUDY THE SCHEDULE

First of all should come a thorough study of the entire show schedule to familiarize the contestant with all the general rules and information, such as the date when all entries must be recorded with the entries committee, the hour when the hall will be open to exhibitors, and the hour when the floor must be cleared for judging.

A special study of the arrangement section is next in order to make sure what all requirements are in the classes in which the novice wishes to enter. These days even the smallest shows are very specific in designating what plant material, type of container, accessories, and background (if any) are permitted in each class, and the exact space allotted to each entry in that class.

It is the business of the classifications chairman to inform an exhibitor of any deviation from these requirements, but sometimes, in the last-minute rush, something slips past her eagle eye.

The judges are—or should be—experienced persons who will be quick to notice, *and to downgrade*, any arrangement which, in any detail, does not comply with the scheduled requirements. We have judged in many shows where excellent arrangements lost out because of failure to comply with some comparatively unimportant limitation.

Particular attention should be paid to such matters as whether or not *accessories* are permitted; whether dried material is considered to be accessory material; if *line* or *mass* is to be stressed; whether a particular kind of container (glass, pottery, metal) is specified; whether a particular color or color harmony is required, and so on.

A typical show schedule is shown on page 259.

Size of Niche or Space

The show schedule will (or should) state the exact *size* of the niche or space in which the entries in each class are to be displayed. It is taken for granted that each arrangement will be *in scale* with this space. If it is so large as to appear crowded, or so small as to seem a bit lost, this will count heavily against it. Here again we have frequently seen arrangements which lost out in close competition, even though in all other respects they would have won ribbons. Frequently in such cases the judges are blamed although the fault is entirely the exhibitor's.

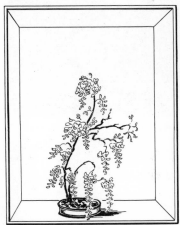

SPACE RELATIONSHIP BETWEEN CONTAINER AND NICHE OR AREA in which it is placed cannot be overemphasized. (1) Niche of correct size and proportion for arrangement (2) Niche too small (3) Niche too large

The safest course to follow, unless from past experience you are familiar with the space specified, is to *construct a niche* of pieces of cardboard, taped together at the edges, of exactly the size called for. If the entry is to be exhibited in a specified space on a table or shelf, mark off the dimensions on the table where you are making your preliminary experiments. You will find this of the greatest assistance in getting your arrangement —base, container, flowers, and accessories (if any)—in scale with the space allotted.

Subtle relationships in color between the vase, the anthuriums, the dried palm fronds, and Deodor "roses," and mastery of the subtleties of handling textures make this a show composition worthy of close study.

Mrs. Robert Kearfott

In this harmonious composition in the Oriental manner, orchids, container, and figurines all contribute to a unified whole.

Mrs. Anne Elizabeth Erhorn

THEME

With these preliminaries out of the way, the next step is to get an *idea* for your arrangement. The schedule will probably imply whether the motif should be expressive (interpretive) or merely decorative (see page 252). In either case you will do well, especially if you are a beginner, to start with a rough—no matter how rough—sketch suggesting the design or pattern you wish to follow. Don't try to put in all the details, but merely the container, the main lines, and the center of interest. These can be corrected until you are satisfied that they comply with the principles of good design—unity, scale, accent, balance, harmony, and rhythm. It will be helpful, too, if at this point you suggest, with color pencils or crayons, the color harmony you may decide to employ. This is especially necessary where a complementary harmony is selected.

Next choose flowers and foliage to provide the forms and colors that will enable you to carry out the design, keeping in mind that the finished arrangement *will be in three dimensions*, instead of following the two-dimensional silhouette you have as a working pattern (see page 76).

Frequently one is limited as to the flowers and foliage available, and then it may be necessary to work the other way round, starting with these and creating a design to accommodate them.

DRY RUN

With these preliminaries attended to, it is advisable—in fact, for the beginner, quite essential—to make, a few days in advance, an arrangement as nearly as possible identical to the one planned for the show. Then if some details do not work out exactly as planned—and almost always there are some which will not—there is an opportunity to change or readjust them. Also, there is then time to examine the finished job at leisure and check it carefully for errors which the judges would be likely to discover. Go over it with your "scale of points" in hand and score it critically as though *you* were a judge. If you have a friend who is more experienced than yourself in this field, ask her to criticize it for you. She will be quite likely to discover faults that have escaped your loving eyes: every baby, you know, to its own mother is the most perfect baby in the world.

Make a *check list* of everything you will want to take to the show, not only plant materials, container, and accessories but also scissors, knife, holders, floral clay, wires, and other tools of the trade mentioned in Chapter 18.

And last, but *not* least, get to the show early. Frequently there is not ample working space for all entrants, and it's a matter of first come, first served. Moreover, things become more and more hectic as "clear-the-floor" time approaches and the chance of some last-minute detail being overlooked is increased.

A final word: if you fail to win an award, do not criticize the judges—at least not out loud. You do not want to get the reputation of being a "kicker." If you do not understand why you failed, make every effort to find out, but do so in a spirit of seeking knowledge, not of attempting to convince the judges—or the show committee—of their lack of it.

Today most judges are well qualified to do their job, which is an unremunerative labor of love. Often they travel long distances, always stand on their feet for hours while judging, and are unflaggingly conscientious in trying to judge fairly. As a general rule they are willing, if requested, to give verbal criticisms of the entries which failed to win, which the clerks jot down on the back of each entry card. These criticisms by the judges are invaluable to the inexperienced exhibitor and should be gratefully received in the spirit in which they were made.

SAMPLE SCHEDULE

RULES AND INFORMATION

Read carefully

1. Exhibitors must find a substitute if unable to exhibit.
2. Entries will be accepted as received, and limited classes will be closed when filled. All entries must be received by the Entries Chairman, Mrs. John Doe, 6 Floral Circle, Maytown, Va., by Monday, May 25. Entries will also be accepted by telephone:
   Rosely 6-3557.
3. Exhibitors may make only one entry in each class.
4. All arrangements must be made and staged by exhibitor.
5. No artificial plant material or coloring of plant material permitted unless specifically so stated in the schedule.
6. Each exhibit shall be passed by the Classifications Committee.
7. Decision of the judges shall be final and judges may withhold any award, if in their opinion the exhibit is not worthy.
8. The hall must be cleared of exhibitors and ready for judging at 11 A.M. on June 1.
9. Exhibits may be removed after 9 P.M. June 1, not before.
10. All due care will be taken, but no responsibility is assumed for loss or breakage.

THEME

Time of Harvest

Classes 1 to 6 to be exhibited in niches 32 inches high, 28 inches wide, 18 inches deep, and 40 inches from floor. Background material, natural monkscloth.

Class 1. *Autumn Riot.* A composition of flowers and/or fruits and/or vegetables in autumn colors in a container or on a tray or base; accessories permitted.

Class 2. *Last Roses.* A composition in silver, pewter, or glass, roses predominating. Dried material and accessories permitted.

Class 3. *Bird Harvest*. A line composition featuring berried shrubs, with other fresh plant material and bird accessories.

Class 4. *November Wind*. A composition to suggest the final leaf fall; weathered wood and other accessories optional.

Class 5. *Night Before Frost*. A line-mass arrangement of living plant material, dahlias predominating.

Class 6. *October Sunset*. Mass arrangement of fresh flowers and autumn foliage in a metal container.

Classes 7 to 12 to be exhibited on tables in spaces 20 inches long by 18 inches deep.

Class 7. *Harvest Moon*. Monochromatic or analogous arrangement of fresh plant material, featuring yellow.

Class 8. *Country Kitchen*. An arrangement of living plant material for a kitchen window sill in autumn; fruits and/or vegetables optional.

Class 9. *Fall Weekend*. An arrangement of autumn flowers and foliage for a guest-room desk or dressing table.

Class 10. *Late Sunshine*. An arrangement of fresh flowers in autumn colors for a coffee table.

Class 11. *Preview of Winter*. An arrangement of dried materials.

Class 12. *New England*. An expressive composition. No restrictions.

Table Arrangements

To be staged on tables 40 inches by 30 inches.

Class 13. An arrangement for an outdoor barbecue in autumn.

Class 14. *Tally Ho*. Composition for a hunt breakfast; accessories required.

Class 15. Table decoration for a children's Halloween party.

Class 16. A composition for a sideboard (buffet) at Thanksgiving; accessories required.

20

FLOWERS AND FOLIAGE FOR ARRANGEMENTS: FROM GARDEN, WINDOW GARDEN, AND FLORIST

The arranger who has no garden of her own is missing half the fun of her favorite hobby.

A very large percentage of all flower arrangements are made for the home—to give everyday enjoyment by brightening the rooms in which we live with fresh flowers and greenery, fragrance and color.

To supply the materials for such decorations, most of us count, in spring, summer, and autumn, upon our gardens. In winter, the florist must be resorted to unless a home greenhouse, sun porch, or window garden is available where house plants and flowers can be grown.

PLAN, BUY, AND PLANT FOR CUTTING

Instead of haphazardly cutting for indoor decoration any flower that happens to be in bloom, it pays to plan ahead and to grow especially for cutting.

Not only the annual and perennial borders but the permanent landscape plantings on the property can be planned and planted with cutting in mind. This is particularly true of a new home, but even in well-established grounds materials especially desirable for the arranger may easily be added.

While the broad-leaved evergreens with their wonderful spring and early summer flowers are the most showy, deciduous flowering shrubs and trees are just as desirable from the arranger's point of view.

Even a few of the larger trees are well worth-while. Paulownia, for instance, provides beautiful, scented lavender flowers on gracefully curving terminal branches, buds which remain like brown velvet throughout the winter before they bloom, and long-lasting, dark brown seed pods of great value to the arranger. The tulip tree, the catalpa, the dogwood, and redbud are other examples.

As for the flowers, the advantages of making at least a few special plantings for cutting are many. You can provide yourself with just the colors you need for the décor of your home. You can grow bold flower forms for focal points and accents, tall spikes for height, and graceful line material to give long, sweeping curves.

And last, but by no means least, you will be sure of a continuity of arrangement material that can never be attained when you merely cut hit or miss from your regular borders of annuals, perennials, bulbs, and shrubs.

A Cutting Garden. You can save time, space, and work by putting these selected plants in a special cutting garden by themselves—and grow better flowers! If you've a vegetable patch, a few short rows there devoted to some annuals, perennials, and bulbs will yield a crop of choice arrangement material.

An alternate plan is to put enough favorite plants in the beds and borders so that any cut blossoms will not be missed.

Among the species and varieties which we have found particularly useful, a number are suggested in the following paragraphs. Unless you have a large garden, you will not want to attempt all of them, especially the first year. But selections from among them will give you a good start toward more dependable material for spring, summer, and fall arrangements.

ANNUALS

The most important thing to consider in ordering annual seeds or buying seedlings is to select *varieties* which will give the most striking effects.

Round Forms. In China asters, for instance, do not be satisfied with an old-fashioned mixture of medium-sized, garishly colored flowers on short stems, but select such varieties as early Bonnie Blue; Giant Crego Enchantress, a salmon-rose, and blush Shell Pink. Also be sure to choose a large, long-stemmed double white. (In areas where wilt is a problem, select wilt-resistant varieties.)

Calendulas for late fall bloom can be had in apricot and cream as well as the usual yellows, golds, and oranges. Sensation cosmos come in wonderful separate colors and bloom weeks before the older sorts. Coltness Hybrid, Unwin Dwarf, and Sunburst dahlias are hard to beat for brilliant color and masses of bloom the first year from seed. Rather like a single orange dahlia is the Mexican sunflower or tithonia. In marigolds, procure the pale ones which blend well with other flowers, such as Miracle Mixture, Man-in-the-Moon, Primrose, and lemon Yellow Climax.

Petunias have made great strides in the past few years. We like the salmon Ballerina, Silver Medal, and Maytime. Red Satin and Fire Dance are only two of the rich reds. The Grandiflora type has large blooms with waved or fringed petals and the spreading branches, each with several handsome blossoms, are naturals for line arrangement. The large full doubles, now to be had in named varieties in white, orchid, salmon, and rose, are big and impressive enough to use as material for the center of interest in an arrangement.

Other annuals to keep in mind are forget-me-not, blue lace-flower, bachelor's buttons, and cynoglossum to supply pure blues; pansies, heliotrope, and torenia for purple and gold.

Celosias may be used fresh or dried, the crested type in the center of a composition, the plumed sorts to give height. Strawflowers, statice, honesty, and globe amaranth also are useful dried as well as fresh.

Godetias in pink, rose, and salmon, and nemesias in all colors but blue are seldom used, but delightful. Salpiglossis is lovely, the delicate, veined and netted blue and silver, or red and gold trumpetlike flowers on frail stems being ideal for graceful,

Mrs. Anne Elizabeth Erhorn

The beginning arranger should learn that it is not necessary to obtain exotic materials in order to create distinctive arrangements. The lovely design above is made with a few flower stalks and foliage rosettes of one echeveria, a common garden subject. The class called for "flowers in a metal container, stressing textural qualities."

drooping lines. And don't forget Bells of Ireland, each stem with a built-in Hogarthian curve.

Verbenas, like petunias, produce charming blooms on long, curving stems and, therefore, can be used for line material, or alone in bowls or low dishes. Nasturtiums lend themselves to similar treatment, especially in glass containers.

For zinnias, order named varieties in separate colors.

To give *height* and long vertical lines, choose *Salvia farinacea*, Imperial larkspur; Tetra or Sentinel snapdragons, and ten- or seven-week stocks.

For *fragrance*, there are candytuft, heliotrope, mignonette, nasturtiums Sensation Mixed, nicotiana, petunias, pinks, stocks, and heat-resistant sweet peas.

Cobaea scandens is an annual vine that has everything: interesting foliage and tendrils, lovely blue or white flowers, and persistent bracts and seed pods.

PERENNIALS

It is hardly necessary, if you are a gardener, to advise you to plant for cutting single and semi-double peonies, Pacific Hybrid delphiniums, Oriental poppies, new roses, modern varieties of day-lilies, and chrysantheumums. If you are a lover of flowers, you are already familiar with these.

Here are a few other things not so commonly grown, but just as valueble to the arranger.

For *height:* Aquilegia, astilbe, campanula, *cimicifuga simplex*, Shirley foxgloves, heuchera, Russell lupine, pentstemon, and thermopsis.

For *large, round forms:* anemone, echinops (globe thistle), anthemis, scabiosa, Shasta daisy, gaillardia, gloriosa daisy, trollius, *aster frikarti.*

For *accents:* Canterbury bell, hollyhock, Oriental poppy, primula, tritoma.

As *fillers:* Gyposphila, statice.

For *fragrance:* dianthus, valeriana (garden heliotrope), viola, tuberose, and yucca.

For *line arrangements:* Siberian, Bearded, and Japanese iris.

Bulbous Flowers

Most of the hardy spring-flowering bulbs are useful as arrangement material, from the shy little chionodoxas through daffodils to fritillarias, tulips, and camassias. In daffodils and tulips you probably have your favorite varieties. Some are longer lasting than others. And for the longest season of bloom for the garden and for cutting, order early-, medium- and late-blooming varieties in both species.

The garden lilies are dramatic and long-lasting in arrangements. Don't miss out on the new hybrids like Enchantment, Fireflame, Valencia, *Speciosum album* and *magnificum*, and the Mid-century, Centifolium, and Auratum hybrids. Few flowers are so spectacular. Grow them for church flowers, show arrangements, wedding flowers, and for prominent positions in the home.

Lycoris squamigera, the hardy amaryllis, is another beautiful, hardy midsummer bloomer.

Then there are the tender bulbs and corms: anemones, calla-lilies, ismenes, gladiolus (especially the primulinus type); montbretias, ranunculus, gloriosa-lilies, bulbous iris, tuberous begonias, and *Lycoris radiata*.

Collecting tender bulbs can be fun if you have a place to store them during their rest period; and no class of plant gives more interesting and dramatic blooms for the delight of the arranger.

House Plants

In winter, a window garden or sun porch may be utilized to grow many flowering plants for use in arrangements. Some of the best are:

African violet	Gardenia
Azalea	Geranium
Begonias, large-leaved	Heliotrope
Begonia semperflorens	Hoya carnosa
Billbergia nutans	Kalanchoe
Camellia	Marguerite

Campanula isophylla
Cypripediums
Epiphyllum cacti
Fuchsia

Orchid
Passion-flower
Primula
Strelitzia
Vriesia

BULBOUS, TUBEROUS

Tender house bulbs	*Hardy, for forcing*	*Tender, for forcing*
Agapanthus	Crocus	Anemone
Amaryllis	Daffodil	Calla-lily
Amarcrinum	French Roman	Cyclamen
Clivia	Hyacinths	Freesia
Hymenocallis	Muscari	Gloriosa-lily
Vallota	Scilla	Ixia
Veltheimia	Tulip	*Lycoris radiata*
		Oxalis
		Narcissi
		Sparaxis

EFFECTIVE FOLIAGE

Accessory foliage is a most important part of arrangement material and cannot be given too much consideration, whether you are growing it in the garden for this purpose, buying it from a florist, or keeping it in the window garden ready for use in the form of foliage plants.

In selecting plants to provide foliage, the following attributes should be considered:

FORM. The shape of the leaves and growing habit of the plant.

COLOR. There is great variation here, from the white of fancy-leaved caladium to the deep red of a canna leaf or the forest green of a rhododendron.

TEXTURE. Foliage can often be chosen to harmonize with the texture of the container: Broadleaf evergreens for glossy pottery or glass and for highly polished metal; rex begonia and other large-leaf begonia leaves for hand-beaten metal, and so on.

*Mrs. Erik A. Thomee
and Mrs. Janet K. Ferguson, Jr.*

COLOR
WITHOUT
FLOWERS

Mrs. Homer Strong

EFFECTIVE
FOLIAGE

Mrs. Constance B. Wallace
Mrs. George A. Lofland

Foliage from florist and window garden are used above; from window garden, garden, and the wild (below) to make effective arrangements without flowers.

Mrs. Constance B. Wallace
Mrs. George A. Lofland

It is not too hard to find interesting foliage, appropriate to each arrangement, and this is true even if no good florist is accessible.

FOLIAGE FROM YOUR GARDEN AND WINDOW GARDEN

At the opening of this chapter, we discussed the possibilities of landscaping, planning, and planting, especially with cut plant material in mind.

Most rewarding and most permanent of such plantings are the *evergreens*, both coniferous and broad-leaved.

Among the *coniferous* trees and shrubs, the yews, hemlocks, junipers, arbor-vitaes, and pines all provide valuable supplementary foliage for the arranger.

Dwarf varieties include the Pfitzer, Andorra, Sargent, and Waukegan junipers; the Dwarf and Spreading Japanese and Kelsey yews; Heath and Berckmann golden arbor-vitae. Of intermediate height are the Graymoss Sawara and Golden Plume sawara falsecypress; Silver redcedar; Umbrella-pine; Upright Japanese, Hatfield, and Hicks' yews; and Sargent Weeping hemlock.

Broad-leaved evergreens are all of use to the arranger, since they provide both flowers and decorative foliage. These include rhododendrons, *Kalmia latifolia*, *Leucothoe catesbaei*, *Pieris japonica* and *floribunda*, and *Mahonia aquifolium*; nandina, photinia, pittosporum, and *Magnolia grandiflora* (tender); evergreen azaleas, boxwood, *pyracantha* (firethorn), *Abelia grandiflora*, *Euonymus Fortunei*, *Hedera Helix*, and all the cotoneasters.

The heathers—*erica*, *calluna*, and *cytisus*—though not broad-leaved, have their peculiar place in arrangement. Scotch broom has probably been more widely used as line material by arrangers than any other one plant; and other members of the family are almost equally valuable.

FOLIAGE FOR ARRANGEMENT (ABOVE) *House Plants* (top, left to right): *isoloma, maranta, calathea, spotted begonia;* (second row): *monstera, abutilon, Schefflera, snail begonia;* (third row): *tibouchina, silver-leaved McNutt geranium, fatsia;* (bottom row): *scented geranium, zonal geranium.* (BELOW) *Outdoor Plants* (top, left to right): *ismene, hellebore, Magnolia glauca, iris;* (center): *Ghent azalea;* (bottom, left to right): *sweet cicely, ranunculus, fern.*

Annuals and perennials to plant for foliage for cutting should include:

White and gray-leaved plants like the artemisias, santolina, *Cerastium tomentosum, Echinops Ritro, Hosta Sieboldiana, Stachys lanata, Veronica incana,* all perennial; and annual sideritis and senecio.

Bluish *Baptisia australis, Bocconia cordata, Hosta Sieboldiana,* all perennial.

Glossy *chrysanthemum nipponicum,* galax, and ginger; *Pachysandra terminalis, Vinca minor.*

Large, handsome leaves of *Acanthus mollis, Hosta plantaginea, Euphorbia epithymoides,* all perennial; and annual castor-oil bean (bronze), amaranthus (red and bronze), perilla (purple and bronze), prickly-poppy (white-veined).

White-blotched or -edged *Hosta undulata* and *Hosta albomarginata,* perennials.

The many variegated forms and colors of coleus in pink and green, crimson and green, white and green, and other combinations.

Fernlike foliage of aquilegia, dicentra, and meadow rue. Fern fronds in variety.

Annual vines: *Cobaea scandens,* Kenilworth ivy.

Perennial vines: ampelopsis, clematis, *Hedera Helix* (ivy) in variety, climbing hydrangea, trumpet vine, wisteria.

Bulb foliage, Hardy: Daffodil, tulip, iris.

Tender: Amaryllis, caladium, hymenocallis (ismene), tuberous begonia, veltheimia.

Deciduous trees: Copper beech, Chinese chestnut, Japanese maple, oak, sassafras, tulip tree.

Vegetables: Rhubarb, chard, kale.

HOUSE-PLANT FOLIAGE FROM THE WINDOW GARDEN

The best and least expensive source of supplementary foliage for arrangements in winter is a collection of semitropical and other house plants in your window garden or sun porch. Some

Good news for arrangers who like carnations! A new branching type, with bouquetlike sprays of several flowers and buds, ideal for long-lasting arrangements. Photo above was taken the day before Christmas; the one below—of the same flowers—the day after New Year's.

of them give a dividend of flowers sometime during the winter and these are marked with an *. Others are grown for their foliage alone.

Amaryllis *	Echeveria *
Anthurium *	Gardenia *
Aspidistra	Grape-ivy
Aucuba	Holly Fern
Begonia, large-leaved *	Lemon-verbena
Billbergia *	Maranta
Bird's-nest Fern	Monstera
Caladium	Oxalis *
Calla-lily *	Pandanus
Camellia *	Pelargonium (scented-leaved)
Croton	Peperomia
Cryptanthus	Philodendron, in variety
Dieffenbachia	Strelitzia *
Dracaena	Veltheimia *

FLORISTS' MATERIAL

If and when you buy florists' flowers, it is sensible to know something about what should be available in the market at the time. Consult the list in Chapter 23 and note what is seasonal. After a little experience, you will learn the price range and manage somehow to content yourself with what you can afford. If roses are $20 a dozen, snapdragons and iris may have to do. But of course the price of roses—and other flowers, too—varies with the season and even with growing conditions in that particular season. The wholesalers try to grow crops to mature for the big holidays and "special" days (like Mother's Day), and if cloudy weather or other difficulties hold them back so that they miss their objective, the market may be glutted with roses, carnations, or gladiolus a week after Christmas, Memorial Day, or some other special season. It is then that you can buy first-class cut flowers very cheaply. It is wise to ask your florist to inform you when such gluts occur. You may be able to profit by them.

And that brings us to the florist. It pays to deal with one reliable firm. If you can find a good man in a convenient spot, give him your regular trade. If you are a good planner, you will decide several days in advance what flowers you want and, after ascertaining what they will cost, order them. Give him a second choice, in case he fails to obtain the original flowers selected.

Discuss your decoration problems with him, too. Tell him how much your budget allows for flowers and ask him to keep you informed of any special bargains which he thinks might interest you. Above all, in the beginning establish the fact that you must have *fresh* flowers at all times—that stale material sold to you as fresh will result at once in your taking your trade elsewhere.

By establishing permanent and intelligent relations with your florist, you have a real ally—one who knows flowers, who can tell you how long each should last, and who can often suggest substitutes when what you want is not to be had.

What to Buy. Among the most reliable cut flowers—those which give the most show and longest life for their price—are gladiolus and snapdragons, which can start out in tall vases and be cut down as they lose their lower florets until they end in low vases or as floating arrangements. These two flowers, being grown in many parts of the country the year round, are never prohibitively high in price. When snapdragons are not satisfactory or available to give height to your bouquets, substitute stocks, heather, or stephanotis. Chrysanthemums are probably the longest lasting of any florists' flower, with the possible exception of mimosa, which dries without losing form and color. Some small-flowered mums do almost the same thing.

First-quality carnations are long-lasting also, but for just that reason they are often sold after they have passed their prime. Be sure your carnations are fresh; if they seem suspiciously cheap in price, beware! When possible, we always get the new Elegance type, each stem of which is a spray of four to six flowers and buds which open gradually over a long period. (See illustration, page 273.)

Roses are always high-priced, but for arrangements, medium or even short-stemmed grades often are better than "firsts" *if* they are fresh.

Sweet peas and freesias are short-lived, but are deliciously fragrant.

For modern compositions strelitzias, tritomas, foxtail-lilies, anthuriums, nerines, callas, amaryllis, and true lilies of many sorts are often available. At least some of these can be had at any time of year.

For the table, select orchids, camellias, or gardenias if your taste is exotic or, if simple, gerberas, carnations, or roses.

Don't forget the gay pageant of forced bulbous flowers when planning arrangements for late winter and early spring. To go with them, lilac and less expensive forced shrubs like pussy willow or blooming fruit branches are available.

Foliage from the Florist

From the florist, for show arrangements and really impressive compositions for use at home, you can secure, by ordering in advance, glossy dark magnolia leaves, eucalyptus, *pittosporum*, cypress, and the foliage of callas, strelitzias, arums, and spathiphyllum. Leaves of dracaena, and of the white-veined fancy-leaved caladiums are striking, as are also the colored forms. Sometimes such broad-leaf evergreens as photinia, mahonia, loquat, and camellia are available.

Do not accept the useless asparagus fern, which is sent with most flowers. Ask for huckleberry, galax, or smilax instead. In autumn all florists carry red oak leaves. These may work into a fall arrangement and prove very useful indeed.

Most florists stock, in winter at least, rhododendron and laurel foliage, and often pine and cedar branches. These are helpful in making semipermanent home arrangements to be used with successive lots of fresh flowers to give emphasis.

Toward spring you can order pussy willows and branches of spring-flowering shrubs to work into arrangements of spring bulbs.

21

TREASURE TROVE OF WILD FLOWERS

From the moment in early spring when the spicebush shows its golden blossoms along bare branches to November when witch-hazel puts on her out-of-season display, there is a wealth of wild material to be had for the cutting, if conservation laws permit. Failing that permission, many people think it worthwhile to grow wildlings in their gardens for careful and prescribed cutting, since many of these make outstanding arrangement material.

SPRING-FLOWERING SHRUBS. This pageant, which starts with pussy willow and spicebush, continues with the alders, bearing their charming catkins, the high-bush blueberries, shaking their rosy bells, dogwood, honeysuckles, viburnums, chokecherries, and shadblow (*Amelanchier*).

In the West and parts of the South, the field is much richer, yielding spiraeas, ceanothus, philadelphus, and the crataeguses, among many others.

As the season advances, the broadleaf evergreens put on their show together with deciduous azaleas. Among the most widely available are rhododendron, laurel (kalmia), and leucothoe.

In the South or West, evergreen ceanothus, broom, azaleas, magnolias, mahonia, pieris, and myrica (or wax myrtle) are added, to name but a few.

FLOWERING TREES. For really distinctive arrangements, try the flowers and foliage of the dignified tulip tree, the blooms and foliage of catalpa, and the sweet-scented violet flowers of paulownia. In the South there are the silver-bell tree and the

Mrs. John R. Bear

Often it is desirable to have arrangements or compositions that will last for more than a few days, especially those for home decoration. An easy way of doing this is to use small plants—with their roots—from the wild, or crocuses or grape-hyacinths from the garden, placing them in damp moss or peatmoss. With long sprays of flowering shrubs or pussy willows placed in water, such an arrangement will last a long time.

deciduous magnolias, many of which are also to be found in the North.

Wild shrubs which are good autumnal arrangement subjects because of foliage color or berries, or both, include spicebush, blueberry, dogwood, bayberry, cranberry-bush (*Viburnum triloba*), sassafras, snowberry, Virginia creeper, red elderberry, and winterberry (*Ilex verticillata*). Many of the viburnums less showy than cranberry-bush still bear red or blue berries which hang on quite well, and most of these charming shrubs turn lovely plum red with or before the first frost.

WOODLAND WILD FLOWERS. It pays to grow such wildlings as Jack-in-the-pulpit, bleeding heart, Dutchman's breeches, squirrel corn, and cypripediums for judicious use in arrangements. For daintier motifs, try columbine, foamflower, violet, marsh-marigold, and woodland ferns. Skunk cabbage blooms can be collected freely and make striking material. Later in the season come the wood lily (*Lilium philadelphicum*), the Turk's cap (*L. superbum*), the lobelias, including the scarlet cardinal flower, and the striking red and white baneberries. Foliage, flowers, and berries of clintonia are all beautiful.

IN THE FIELDS, as summer advances, we find milkweeds, meadowsweet, steeplebush, meadow rue, black-eyed Susan, lupines, gentians, Queen Anne's lace, mallows, and orange butterfly weed.

With autumn come asters, goldenrods, Joe Pye weed, iron weed, sunflowers, and clematis, together with boneset, false foxglove, and purple gerardia.

In making wild-flower arrangements do not become delirious with all the material available. Restrain yourself and be selective. Otherwise you are apt to have a vase of specimens demonstrating how many species you can collect rather than a well-designed arrangement composed of wildlings. The same principles apply to wild-flower arrangements as are followed in other work with cut flowers. As a rule, the simpler the design when using wild material, the more effective. Many artists convert interesting pieces of tree root, bark, or driftwood into

FROM THE WILD. Dried and fresh material from the swamps (cattails, skunk cabbage foliage and blossoms), mixed with a little creative imagination, resulted in this charming show arrangement.

Mrs. Wendell Kilmer

Treasure trove from the Maine woods, gathered on a stroll by the authors, produced this composition which survived a long trip home and—with an occasional sprinkling—remained fresh for weeks. (That time we got there ahead of the bulldozers!)

containers for such flowers. These seem more appropriate than most other vases or dishes. A metal container for water is secreted somewhere in the heart of the piece of wood. If a conventional container is used, it should be of plain design: a bean pot, pickle jar, earthen pitcher, or low Oriental dish of neutral color and without decoration.

Mrs. John Potter

Small ferns, Jack-in-the-pulpits, and other wildlings, with roots attached, will remain fresh for many days if placed in plenty of water.

And now another word about conservation before closing this discussion of wildlings. Conservation laws had to be made to save our dwindling natives, and those laws must be obeyed by all. However, if wild material can be taken without damage or loss of plants, from a plot of ground owned by the exhibitor, we cannot see why it should be the duty of any flower-show official to disqualify an arrangement of wildlings made from such lawfully acquired material. We all know that the conservation laws were made for vandals who sold truck loads of holly, azalea, laurel, and other wild material for commercial purposes. Unthinking and uneducated individuals also raided the woods and hedgerows, taking more than they could use or keep in good condition. It is ridiculous, however, to believe that one spray of dogwood or one or two cypripedium blooms, selected carefully by a flower-arrangement artist from her own grounds, could possibly imperil the country's supply of wild flowers. On the contrary, by displaying this material in a fine arrangement she is teaching others to appreciate the fineness and the beauty of native material, and by encouraging its cultivation, actually helping conservation.

22

DRIED PLANT MATERIALS:
HOW TO SELECT, PRESERVE, AND ARRANGE THEM

Those who wish to specialize in arranging dried material have much to learn and many hours of discovery and enjoyment before them.

The range of materials is almost inexhaustible, for ingenious artists are constantly adding to it. The following lists are not intended to be all-inclusive, but rather to be typical. Alert interest will suggest to the reader many more items in each group.

Classes featuring such material fall into four general categories:

1. DRIFTWOOD AND DRIED BARE BRANCHES of trees, shrubs, and vines. These may be left in their natural state; waxed and rubbed; or polished to an old bone finish with the dull blade of a silver knife.
2. DRIED SEEDS, PODS, CONES, AND BERRIES:
    (a) On their own long stems, for line work, as ornamental grasses, fertile fern fronds, dock heads, sea oats, ripe wheat and milkweed pods, cattails, lotus, iris and lily seed heads, leek and onion seed heads.
    (b) On short stems, clustered together for use as accent or focal material. Examples are nuts, acorns, chinaberries, pyracantha berries, coniferous cones, pods of Paulownia, locust, Kentucky coffee tree, trumpet vine, wisteria, magnolia, eucalyptus, jacaranda, agave, castor bean, unicorn plant (*proboscidea*), and *Cobaea scandens*.

3. DRIED FOLIAGE, most of which can be preserved by the glycerin method later described.

    (A) On its own stems or branches as leaves of beech, Chinese chestnut, oak, magnolia, elaeagnus, blueberry, leucothoe, bamboo, and English ivy.

    (B) Broad or straplike leaves: aspidistra, ti, sea-grape, strelitzia, pandanus, fiddle-leaved rubber plant, sansevieria, gladiolus, iris, calla, mullein, and the humble cabbage.

4. FLOWERS:

    (A) Easily dried by hanging upside down in dark, as

Acacia	Goldenrod
Achillea	Heather
Artemisia	Honesty
Astilbe	Lavender
Bells-of-Ireland	Meadow rue
Catanache	Peony
Celosia	Salvia
Everlasting	Statice

    (B) Fragile, on one-inch stems, to be dried in sand or borax and corn meal:

Anemone	Larkspur
Aster	Lilac
Buddleia	Lupine
Calendula	Marigold
Chrysanthemum	Minor bulbs
Clematis	Pansy
Columbine	Poppy
Cosmos	Rose
Daffodil	Rudbeckia
Dahlia	Scabiosa
Delphinium	Shasta Daisy
Dianthus	Spiraea
Dicentra	Sunflower
Fuchsia	Tulip
Heuchera	Viola
Iberis	Zinnia

Esther C. Grayson

*DRIED ARRANGE-
MENTS. Interesting forms
and colors may be found in
all sorts of plant materials
and dried and saved for
winter decoration. Flower
heads of leeks here provide
unusual effect.*

Mrs. Erik A. Thomee

Mrs. Anne Elizabeth Erhorn

For Seaside Effects	For Arrangements
Crabs	Bumblebees
Sea horses	Butterflies
Starfish	Birds' nests
Shells, in variety	Birds' eggs
Sea fans	Dragonflies
Corals	Rocks
Cork floats	Dried mosses
Driftwood	Dried lichens
Seaweeds, dried	Fungi

DRYING, PRESERVING, PRESSING

DRYING

By hanging material upside down. Everlastings and other flowers which dry easily (see List 4-A) may simply be hung upside down from lines or coat hangers, not touching each other, preferably in a dark place which is dry and airy. If dried in the light, much more of their natural colors will be lost.

With Sea Sand; or a Mixture of ½ *Borax,* ½ *Corn Meal.* Fragile blooms of delicate colors (see List 4-B) are best dried by covering them a few days to several weeks, depending on the material, with fine, clean sea sand or a half-and-half mixture of sifted borax and fine corn meal.

A layer of the drying material is placed in the bottom of a cardboard box. Flowers, from the stems of which all foliage has been stripped, are gently placed on this, face down or face up, and the sand or borax mixture is very gently poured around the heads until they are covered.

Sprays like delphinium, larkspur, lupine, and heuchera are laid lengthwise in a long box on a layer of drying material. The entire sprays are then gently covered with the same mixture.

In drying trumpet-shaped flowers like daffodils, trumpet-lilies, datura, and althea, the blooms should be carefully filled with the drying material to help preserve the natural shapes.

With very double blossoms like peonies and double roses,

cotton or sand may be packed in the interstices to keep the globular forms from collapsing during the drying process.

PRESSING

For blooms, autumn leaves, and other foliage to be used in framed still lifes or on panels, material may be pressed between several thicknesses of newspaper and then weighted with heavy books.

GLYCERIN METHOD

Most types of foliage (see Lists 3-A and B) are permanently and beautifully preserved by placing 4 to 5 inches of the stems of cut sprays in jars containing a mixture of ⅓ glycerin and ⅔ water. The ends of woody stems are crushed to help the process of absorption, and materials are left in the mixture until it has been absorbed to the tips of the leaves. As soon as this occurs the materials are promptly removed and hung upside down until fully cured, when they may be packed in florists' boxes. In many cases this treatment changes the natural color of leaves but gives them a smooth, silky texture which is most attractive. Two great advantages are that they are not as brittle as when naturally dried and their stems may be placed in water without injury when they are combined with fresh plant material.

In all methods of drying, pressing, and preserving, the time factor is an uncertain one. Examine blooms in sand or borax and remove them as soon as they seem to be completely dried. They may then be stored upright in jars or with the stems stuck in blocks of Styrofoam, or laid away between layers of wax paper in florists' boxes. In either case they should be carefully guarded from dust. Pressed flowers should be removed from their weighted papers as soon as they are dry and before they lose color. They can then be stored between layers of waxed paper in shallow boxes.

Artificial stems may be added before storing, or when the flowers are wanted for an arrangement. A dried hollow stem may be slipped over the old stem stump and, if necessary, fastened with floral tape. If just the right size can be found, however, the stump can be pushed up snugly *inside* the hollow false stem so that it holds firmly.

EXOTIC DRIED MATERIAL AND ACCESSORIES AVAILABLE AT FLOWER ARRANGERS' SUPPLY SHOPS

Dried Plants	Accessories
Agave leaves	Bases
seed pods	
Alpine thistle	Burls
Aspidistra leaves	Clay, floral
Bottle-tree pods	Containers
Desert-spoon	Coral
Devil's-claw	Corsage supplies
Eucalyptus pods tips	Cork
Kashmir thistle	Cypress knees
Lotus pods	Driftwood
Magnolia leaves	Glass slag or chips
Maidenhair fern	Marbles
Okra pods	Mats, bamboo
Palm hearts	Philippine
Palm plumes	Netting, fish
Pine cones	Oasis
Scotch broom	Paraffin
Sea-grape leaves	Plant ties
Sea-oats	Rafts, bamboo
Wheat	Shears
Wood-roses,	Shells
Deodor	Styrofoam
Hawaiian	Water pics
Miniature	Wax, plastic
Indian	Wire, florist

Dried materials, mounted on plyboard panels, grass mats, or fabrics, make interesting wall decorations. Here, wild seashore plants, seaweeds, seed pods, and sea shells have been combined in pleasing designs.

Esther C. Grayson

Techniques

Arrangements. Driftwood, dried branches, embryo palm hearts, and some other dried hardwood materials are so heavy as to present real problems to the arranger.

Heavy branches may be held in place with the type of clay used by florists for the purpose. It dries absolutely hard but cannot be placed in water. Years ago when it first came on the market, a florist told me it was waterproof. Before a large audience I arranged a branch of driftwood in a low container, added water and a focal center of fresh flowers and foliage. Placed on display, the driftwood first bowed slowly to the audience—and then toppled over on the table! My face was red, and the florist, who was in the audience, did not know which way to look.

Since then I prefer to set heavy material in a needle-point holder firmly attached to the bottom of the container and then to reinforce it with large lumps of waterproof floral clay worked into the holder and up around the base of the branches.

The feather lightness of most dried material makes it easy to arrange and move from place to place. Containers should be partly filled with vermiculite, or shredded Styrofoam, both of which are very light. Stems can then be firmly set in the medium. When low dishes are used, needle-point holders are preferable, but these, of course, must be covered with foliage, pebbles, or rocks.

A supply of extra stems, with wire, Twistems, and/or pipe cleaners, make it possible to add stem lengths as needed. Pipe cleaners are useful in making a curving stem which will not be visible in the finished arrangement.

Many dried blossoms are so fragile that they shatter at a rough touch. Handle them very gently, and if necessary re-stick with rubber cement petals which drop off.

When making miniatures, small tweezers are a great help in

placing material; and a pair of long, slim olive tongs may be used in the same way for larger material in making still lifes and panels.

Still Lifes, Collages, Panels, Table Tops, Paper Weights

In these phases of the art, plant material is permanently fastened to its background.

Duco or an immediate-contact glue containing rubber for heavy branches are the best stickers for the purpose.

Material may be tentatively laid on the background to try out the design; or a drawing may be lightly sketched on the board or fabric and the plant material superimposed on it.

If a glass-covered frame or paperweight is to go over the design, its thickness must be kept within the available space between background and glass.

In making panels on wood, where cones, pods, sprays, shells, and so on are used in rather formal, clean-cut designs, strive for an effect of wood carved in bas-relief. Plant material to be used for this purpose, before or after being mounted, should be shellacked or sprayed with clear plastic.

23

ARRANGEMENTS AROUND THE YEAR

Each season brings its quota of flowers which are particularly desirable for indoor decoration. It is helpful to the arranger to know at a glance what is or could be available in any particular month.

First of all, there are the florists' flowers which she can buy. Better transportation has made it possible for florists to offer certain items like snapdragons and gladiolus every month in the year. In the winter they come from the South. In summer they are grown in the North. Other cut flowers are strictly seasonal, like forced spring-flowering bulbs. By consulting the lists in this chapter, you can ascertain in a moment just what flowers can be purchased in any month. In this way it will be possible for you to plan your arrangement before purchasing flowers, since you know in advance what is in the market.

In the same way, a study of the lists of garden and window-garden plants will tell you what you have, or can grow if you wish, to keep up a constant supply of flowers and foliage for arrangements throughout the year.

Those of us who are fortunate enough to have gardens can save materially by planning and planting to provide flowers for cutting through a long season. These may be supplemented by foliage, berries, and such plants as witch-hazel and hellebore in winter.

It is not enough for the enthusiastic arranger to have a garden of profuse bloom. To be really efficient she should plan and plant with arrangements especially in mind. Many lovely garden flowers are not ideal for cutting. Among these are fleeting blooms like day-lilies and those which close at night like evening primrose. Study the monthly lists and plan to plant accordingly. Make yours an arranger's garden.

Still another rich source of flower-arrangement material may be found among house plants. It is fun to visit local greenhouses and look up growers who offer unusual items. Then, too, there are the tender winter-flowering bulbs which can be purchased at the same time as the hardy bulbs, planted in pots, and brought to winter bloom for use in arrangements. A few blooms, purchased or produced in the window garden, can be supplemented by the showy foliage of begonias, dracaenas, dieffenbachias, and so on. I keep one spotted begonia plant in a large pot especially for use in winter arrangements. The beautiful foliage with rose-color reverse sides and silver spots on top goes well with any number of flowers. In addition, the plant produces showy clusters of large rose-pink blooms. Many women who arrange flowers frequently keep such plants in reserve for supplementary material. Though the symmetry of such specimens may be destroyed by cutting so that they have to be kept like Cinderellas in a kitchen window or other out-of-the-way corner, they are nonetheless rewarding in the work they do toward beautifying the home.

It will pay you to consult the following lists carefully and to keep them always available for ready reference.

JANUARY

Cut Flowers

Acacia
Agapanthus
Amaryllis
Anemone
Anthurium
Antirrhinum
Begonias
Bouvardia
Buddleia
Calanthe
Calendula
Calla-lily
Camellia
Carnation
Cornflower
Daffodil
Delphinium

Euphorbia
Freesia
Gardenia
Gerbera
Gladiolus
Gloriosa-lily
Heather
Iris, bulbous
Lilac
Lilies:
   Croft
   Auratum
   Longiflorum
   Others in season
Lily-of-the-valley
Muscari

Nerine
Orchids:
   Cattleya
   Cypripedium
   Oncidium
   Phalaenopsis
   Vanda
Pansy
Poppy
Primula
Pyrethrum
Ranunculus
Rose
Strelitzia
Sweet pea
Tulip
Violet

Plants

Azalea
Cyclamen
Daffodil
Fuchsia

Gardenia
Geranium

Hyacinth
Kalanchoe
Marguerite
Primula

Evergreens, broad-leaf   Evergreens, coniferous

Amaryllis
Begonias, winter-blooming
Calla-lily   Freesia

Kalanchoe
Veltheimia
Foliage plants

JANUARY. Callas, easily arranged, are effective and extra long-lasting.

FEBRUARY

Cut Flowers

Acacia
Amaryllis
Anemone
Anthurium
Antirrhinum
Arbutus
Bouvardia
Buddleia
Calendula
Calla-lily
Camellia
Carnation
Cornflower
Daffodil
Euphorbia

Freesia
Gardenia

Gladiolus
Gloriosa-lily
Heather
Iris, bulbous
Lace-flower
Lilac
Lilies, various
Lily-of-the-valley
Mignonette
Montbretia

Muscari
Nerine
Orchids, various
Pansy
Poppy
Primula
Pyrethrum
Ranunculus
Rose
Stephanotis
Stock
Strelitzia
Sweet pea
Tulip
Violet

Plants

Begonia
Calceolaria
Cineraria
Cyclamen

Daffodil
Fuchsia
Gardenia
Hyacinth

Marguerite
Primula
Tulip

Mrs. Bertram Flory, Jr.

FEBRUARY. A few florists' flowers—stocks, roses, freesias, and ranunculus.

MARCH

Cut Flowers

Acacia
Agapanthus
Amaryllis
Anemone
Arbutus
Calendula
Calla-lily
Camellia
Carnation
Cornflower
Daphne
Freesia
Gerbera

Gladiolus
Gloriosa-lily
Heather
Iris, bulbous
Lilac
Lilies, various
Lily-of-the-valley
Mignonette
Montbretia
Muscari
Orchids, various

Pansy
Poppy
Primula
Pyrethrum
Ranunculus
Rose
Scabiosa
Stephanotis
Stock
Strelitzia
Sweet pea
Tulip
Violet

Plants

Astilbe
Begonia
Cyclamen
Daffodil

Fuchsia
Geranium
Hyacinth

Hydrangea
Lilies, Easter
Rose
Tulip

Crocus
Flowering shrub branches (forced)
Flowering fruit branches (forced)

Pussy willow
Snowdrop
Spring-flowering bulbs

MARCH. From the window garden: geraniums with their own foliage.

APRIL

Cut Flowers

Amaryllis
Anemone
Anthurium
Antirrhinum
Arbutus
Calendula
Calla-lily
Carnation
Cornflower
Daffodil
Daphne
Delphinium

Freesia
Gardenia
Gerbera
Gladiolus
Gloriosa-lily
Gypsophila
Iris, bulbous
Lilac
Lilies, various
Lupine
Mignonette
Montbretia

Muscari
Nasturtium
Orchids, various
Pansy
Primula
Rose
Scabiosa
Stephanotis
Stock
Strelitzia
Tulip
Violet

Plants

Astilbe
Begonia
Daffodil
Fuchsia

Geranium
Heliotrope
Hyacinth

Hydrangea
Lilies, Easter
Rose
Tulip

Azalea
Chionodoxa
Crocus
Daffodil
Fritillaria

Leucothoe
Magnolia
Muscari
Primula
Scilla

Shrubs, flowering
Squill
Trollius
Tulips (species and
species hybrids)

Mrs. Willard Schneider

APRIL. Spring at last—with daffodils, forsythia, and pussy willows.

MAY

Cut Flowers

Anemone
Anthurium
Antirrhinum
Aquilegia
Bouvardia
Buddleia
Calendula
Calla-lily
Carnation
Cornflower
Daffodil
Delphinium
Freesia

Gardenia
Gerbera
Gladiolus
Gloriosa-lily
Iris, bulbous
Lilac
Lilies, various
Lily-of-the-valley
Lupine
Mignonette
Montbretia
Muscari
Nasturtium

Orchids, various
Pansy
Peony
Primula
Rose
Scabiosa
Stephanotis
Stock
Sweet pea
Tulip
Violet
Water-lily
Zinnia

Plants

Begonia
Fuchsia

Heliotrope

Geranium
Hyacinth

Aquilegia
Azalea
Dianthus
Dicentra
Digitalis
Doronicum
Gaillardia
Geum
Heuchera
Iris
Kalmia
Lily-of-the-valley

Myosotis
Pansy
Peony
Phlox divaricata
Rhododendron
Shrubs, flowering
Statice
Trollius
Tulip
Viola
Violet
Wisteria

MAY. Tulips, informally arranged to counteract their usual stiff appearance when used as cut flowers.

JUNE

Cut Flowers

Anthurium
Antirrhinum
Aquilegia
Aster, China
Bouvardia
Buddleia
Calendula
Calla-lily
Carnation
Cornflower
Dahlia
Delphinium
Gaillardia
Gardenia

Gerbera
Gladiolus
Gloriosa-lily
Gypsophila
Larkspur
Lilies, various
Lily-of-the-valley
Lupine
Marguerite
Marigold
Mignonette
Nasturtium
Orchids, various

Pansy
Peony
Primula
Pyrethrum
Ranunculus
Rose
Scabiosa
Shasta Daisy
Stock
Sweet pea
Tritoma
Tuberose
Water-lily
Zinnia

Plants

Begonia

Fuchsia

Geraniums

Allium
Antirrhinum
Astilbe
Campanula
Coreopsis
Delphinium
Dianthus
Digitalis
Dimorphotheca

Gaillardia
Heuchera
Iris
Ismene
Kalmia
Lily, Madonna
Myosotis
Lupine
Penstemon

Peony
Poppy
Pyrethrum
Rhododendron
Rose
Rudbeckia
Scabiosa
Sweet pea
Yucca

Mrs. Claire Stickles

JUNE. Roses, indoors as well as out.

JULY

Cut Flowers

Agapanthus
Alstroemeria
Anthurium
Antirrhinum
Aquilegia
Aster, China
Bouvardia
Carnation
Clivia
Cornflower
Dahlia
Delphinium

Eucharis
Gardenia
Gerbera
Gladiolus
Gloriosa-lily
Gypsophila
Iris, Japanese
Larkspur
Liatris
Lilies, various
Lily-of-the-valley
Marguerite

Mignonette
Pansy
Primula
Pyrethrum
Ranunculus
Rose
Scabiosa
Shasta Daisy
Stock
Sweet pea
Tritoma
Tuberose

Plants

Begonia

Fuchsia

Geranium

Abelia
Aconitum
Anthemis
Arctotis
Butterfly Weed
Campanula
Centaurea
Clematis
Coreopsis
Dahlia
Delphinium
Dianthus
Digitalis
Dimorphotheca

Echinops
Fuchsia
Gaillardia
Geranium
Geum
Gladiolus
Gypsophila
Iris, Japanese
Lilies
Marigold
Nasturtium
Petunia
Phlox

Platycodon
Poppy
Rose
Salvia farinacea
Salpiglossis
Santolina
Scabiosa
Shasta Daisy
Sweet pea, annual
Sweet pea, perennial
Tritoma
Verbena
Viola
Zinnia

Esther C. Grayson

JULY. Lilies arrange themselves.

AUGUST

FROM THE FLORIST
Cut Flowers

Agapanthus
Alstroemeria
Anthurium
Antirrhinum
Aster, China
Celosia
Chrysanthemum
Clivia
Cornflower
Dahlia
Delphinium
Eucharis

Gaillardia
Gardenia
Gerbera
Gladiolus
Gloriosa-lily
Gypsophila
Larkspur
Liatris
Lilies, various
Lily-of-the-valley

Marguerite
Marigold
Mignonette
Nasturtium
Nigella
Pyrethrum
Rose
Scabiosa
Shasta Daisy
Tritoma
Tuberose
Zinnia

Plants

Begonias

Geraniums

FROM THE GARDEN

Anthemis
Antirrhinum
Asters, China
Begonia, Tuberous
Calendula
Campanula
Celosia
Centaurea
Cosmos
Dahlias
Delphinium
Echinops
Geranium
Globe Artichoke
Gladiolus

Gloriosa Daisy
Heliotrope
Hosta
Lace-flower
Lantana
Larkspur
Leek blossoms
Liatris
Lily
Lupine
Lycoris
Marigold
Moonflower
Montbretia
Mignonette

Nasturtium
Onion blossoms
Petunia
Phlox, Garden
Rose
Rudbeckia
Salpiglossis
Salvia
Stock
Stokesia
Tritoma
Santolina
Sunflower
Verbena
Zinnia

AUGUST. Day-lilies, now available in an ever-widening range of colors, provide blooms over a long period.

SEPTEMBER

FROM THE FLORIST
Cut Flowers

Agapanthus	Delphinium	Marigold
Alstroemeria	Gardenia	Physalis
Anthurium	Gerbera	Rose
Antirrhinum	Gladiolus	Scabiosa
Aster, China	Gloriosa-lily	Shasta Daisy
Celosia	Larkspur	Strelitzia
Chrysanthemum	Liatris	Tritoma
Cornflower	Lilies, various	Tuberose
Dahlia	Lily-of-the-valley	Zinnia

Plants

Begonia		Geranium
Chrysanthemum	Gardenia	Shrimp Plant

FROM THE GARDEN

Aconitum	Clematis	Marigold
Anemones,	*Cobaea scandens*	Moonflower
Japanese	Cosmos	Myosotis
Antirrhinum	Dahlia	Nasturtium
Artemesia	Delphinium	Petunia
Aster, China	Dianthus	Salvia
Aster, hardy	Eupatorium	Santolina
Calendula	Gaillardia	Shrubs, berried
Campanula	Gladiolus	Sunflower
Catananche	Globe Artichoke	Verbena
Celosia	Gloriosa Daisy	Viola
Chrysanthemum	Lilies, various	Zinnia

SEPTEMBER. Late-summer bounty of sunflowers, dwarf dahlias, cushion chrysanthemums, zinnias, corn, and sumac arranged in a gourd by an artist whose name has escaped the photographer.

OCTOBER

FROM THE FLORIST
Cut Flowers

Antirrhinum
Bouvardia
Calla-lily
Carnation
Chrysanthemum
Cornflower
Dahlia
Delphinium

Gardenia
Gerbera
Gladiolus
Gloriosa-lily
Liatris
Lilies, various
Lily-of-the-valley

Orchids, various
Physalis
Rose
Stephanotis
Strelitzia
Tritoma
Tuberose
Zinnia

Plants

Chrysanthemum
Gardenia

Geranium
Shrimp Plant

FROM THE GARDEN

Aster, China
Aster, hardy
Calendula
Chrysanthemum
Clematis

Cobaea scandens
Colchicum
Cosmos
Eupatorium

Marigold
Petunia
Rose
Shrubs, berried
Zinnia

Esther C. Grayson

OCTOBER. *Chrysanthemums, undisputed queens of the late-
flower borders, are as long-lasting and lovely indoors as out.*

NOVEMBER

FROM THE FLORIST
Cut Flowers

Anemone	Euphorbia	Physalis
Anthurium	Gardenia	Primula
Antirrhinum	Gerbera	Pyrethrum
Asters, China	Gladiolus	Ranunculus
Bouvardia	Godetia	Rose
Calla-lily	Heather	Stephanotis
Camellia	Lilies, various	Strelitzia
Carnation	Lily-of-the-valley	Sweet pea
Chrysanthemum	Nerine	Tritoma
Cornflower	Orchids, various	Tuberose

Plants

Azalea		Gardenia
Chrysanthemum	Cyclamen	Geranium

FROM THE GARDEN

Chrysanthemum	Shrubs, berried	Witch-hazel

Everett Feucht

NOVEMBER. *Indian summer, even after Jack Frost has gathered all but the toughest of late flowers, supplies a wealth of decorative material for indoor decoration. Here the first Massachusetts Thanksgiving is suggested.*

DECEMBER

Cut Flowers

Acacia
Anemone
Anthurium
Antirrhinum
Aster, China
Begonia
Bouvardia
Buddleia
Calla-lily
Camellia
Carnation
Chrysanthemum

Cornflower
Daffodils
Delphinium
Euphorbia
Freesia
Gardenia
Gerbera
Gladiolus
Gloriosa-lily
Heather

Lilies, various
Lily-of-the-valley
Nerine
Orchids, various
Pansy
Poppy
Pyrethrum
Ranunculus
Rose
Strelitzia
Sweet pea
Violet

Plants

Azalea
Begonia, Christmas
Cyclamen
Decorative Pepper

Fuchsia
Gardenia

Jerusalem Cherry
Kalanchoe
Poinsettia
Primula

FROM THE GARDEN

Hellebore (Christmas-rose)

FROM THE WINDOW GARDEN

Christmas Cactus
Poinsettia

Cyclamen
Decorative Pepper

Jerusalem Cherry
Kalanchoe

DECEMBER. And even after driving snows have laid their white mantle over lawn and garden, Christmas-roses push up their fragile-looking, but unbelievably enduring, golden-centered chalices to hold the fort into the New Year.

GLOSSARY OF TERMS
USED IN THIS BOOK

Accessory. Object other than fresh plant material, container and base under container; used to enhance arrangement or composition.

Achromatic. Colorless: black; gray.

Advancing Colors. Warm hues from red to yellow.

Arrangement. Plant material organized in a design which follows recognized art principles. Includes container and base on which it stands, and may also include accessories, according to 1958 National Council Directive.

Background. Surface behind and under a composition against which it is viewed.

Balance. Placement of elements to create equilibrium. In flower arrangement, balance is achieved by the use of both actual and visual weight.

  Asymmetrical. Balance without bilateral symmetry.

  Symmetrical. Balance achieved by placing elements which are exactly alike on either side of an imaginary central axis.

Chroma. Intensity of a color or hue.

Complementary Colors. Colors exactly opposite each other on the color wheel.

Composition. A planned design of plant material, container, base, and may also include background fabric and accessories.

Container. Receptacle which holds cut plant material.

Contrast. Use of opposites.

Cool Colors. Receding colors—green to violet.

Decorative. Used to describe floral designs which are not expressive or interpretive.

Design. Elements organized and arranged in an art form.

Distinction. Superiority achieved through craftsmanship, inspiration, and proficiency.

Dominance. In design indicates a controlling element of color, form, texture, and so on.

Dried Material. Genuine, natural plant material which has been preserved by drying.

Driftwood. Water-washed and worn wood.

Entry. One item placed in competition.

Expressive. In relation to flower arrangement, an interpretive composition expressing an idea or developing a theme.

Form. Shape and outline.

Gradation. Gradual change.

Harmonious Colors. Adjacent hues.

Holder. Device to hold plant material in position.

Hue. Any one section of the color wheel, at full chroma.

Intensity. Chroma. The term used instead of chroma in "pigmatic" theory.

Intermediate Hue. Sections of the color wheel not at full chroma, as yellow-green, blue-green, and so on.

Miniature. A very small arrangement, usually three inches over-all.

Monochromatic. Of one color, which may include its tints, shades, and tones.

Neutral Colors. White, gray, black; achromatic colors; or colors which nearly approach gray, as a neutral green.

Niche. A wall recess or open-front box in which to display a floral composition.

Nosegay. Tussy mussy. Tight hand bouquet of fragrant flowers.

Novice. One who enters competitive classes in a flower show for the first time, or who has previously entered but failed to win an award.

Pattern. Outline or silhouette of a composition.

Principle of Design. One of the fundamental precepts of art.

Proportion. Relationship between one part of a design and another.

Receding Colors. Cool hues from green to blue-violet.

Repetition. Repeated use of elements in a design.

Rhythm. As it refers to flower arrangement: frozen motion.

Scale. Size relationship.

Shade. Any color to which black has been added. See page 102.

Silhouette. Pattern.

Texture. The surface structure.

Tint. Any color to which white has been added. See page 102.

Tone. Any color to which gray has been added. See page 102.

Transition. A gradual change from one color, one form, one size, to another or others.

Tussy Mussy. Similar to a nosegay.

Value of Color. Color intensity.

Voids. Spaces between the solid elements in a composition.

Warm Colors. Advancing colors—red to yellow.

SCALES OF POINTS FOR THE AMATEUR FLOWER SHOW

ARTISTIC SECTION

(From *The Handbook for Flower Shows*, Pub. 1957
National Council of State Garden Clubs, Inc.)

Period or Special Theme
  as—Early American,
  Christmas, etc.

Appropriateness to period or theme	20
Design	25
Color	20
Distinction	15
Originality	10
Condition	10
	——
	100

Massed Line Arrangement

Design	30
Color	30
Distinction	20
Suitability of materials	20
	——
	100

Line Arrangement

Design (Rhythm allotted 15 points; other principles 5 points each)	40
Color	15
Restraint	20
Distinction	25
	——
	100

Arrangement of Flowers
  and/or Fruit and/or Vegetables
    Design   30
    Color   20
    Suitability and combination
      of materials   20
    Distinction   20
    Condition   10
                          ———
                         100

Period Bouquet
    Schedule to state which
      century and era.
    Conformance to theme or period   20
    Design   30
    Color   30
    Distinction in selection
      of material   20
                          ———
                         100

Color Study for Various
  Color Organizations
    Analogous; analogous—
      complementary; complementary;
      monochromatic; split-comple-
      mentary; achromatic; triads
    Color   35
    Design   30
    Distinction   20
    Originality   15
                          ———
                         100

In classes where both color
  study and design problems
  are involved. Example: An arrangement using triadic hues.
    Conformance to theme   10
    Design   40
    Color Design   40
    Distinction   10
                          ———
                         100

Design—Expressive, Interpretive

Originality	35
Design	35
Color	20
Distinction	10
	———
	100

Exhibit in Paired Containers
(identical or unalike), as
one design or as a pair, according to schedule—on mantels or other appropriate
settings

Conformance to theme	10
Suitability to placing	25
Design	30
Color	15
Distinction	20
	———
	100

Miniatures and Small Arrangements

Scale	40
Design	30
Color	20
Condition	10
	———
	100

Trays

Color combination of whole	20
Design	35
Distinction	15
Suitability to purpose:	
practicality	10
correctness	10
Condition	10
	———
	100

Niche (Emphasis on Design)

Scale. Relation of all materials to space and to each other	35
Design. Relationship of line, mass, balance, and emphasis	35
Color	30
	———
	100

Corsages—Fresh Plant Material
(Schedule must specify occasion and whether background is provided)

Technique	15
Design	25
Color	15
Suitable combination of material	15
Distinction	20
Condition	10
	———
	100

Corsages—Dried Material
(Schedule must specify occasion and whether background is provided)

Technique	10
Design	30
Color	10
Combination of materials	20
Originality	15
Distinction	15
	———
	100

Nosegays

Perfection of arrangement	30
Color	25
Distinction and originality	30
Fragrance	15
	———
	100

Arrangement in Placement Show*

Design	30
Suitability to placement	25
Suitability of material	20
Distinction	25
	———
	100

Simplified Scales of Points Used by Federated Garden Clubs of New York State, Inc.

Arrangement Classes Without Specific Purpose

Design (all six principles considered)	30
Color (distinctive use of)	20
Suitable relationship of all materials	20
Distinction	10
Originality	10
Condition of all materials	10
	———
	100

Arrangement with a Theme, Title, or Purpose

Design (all six principles considered)	25
Interpretation, suitability	20
Color	15
Relationship	15
Distinction	15
Condition	10
	———
	100

Table Setting Without a Purpose Named

Over-all design of entire table	25
Relationship of all materials	25
Color	20
Perfection of arrangement	20
Condition	10
	———
	100

* See glossary

Table Setting for a Special Occasion or with a Title

Over-all design	25
Relationship of all materials	20
Color	15
Perfection of arrangement or decoration	15
Suitability or interpretation	15
Condition of all materials	10
	100

Note: Though "condition" is not specifically mentioned in all the scales of points given above, condition of material is always important and will be considered by the judges. *Authors.*

HELPFUL BOOKS
ON FLOWER ARRANGEMENT

Chinese Flower Arrangement by H. L. Li, 1959, Van Nostrand.

Color in Flower Arrangement by Adelaide B. Wilson, 1954, M. Barrows & Co., Inc., New York.

Complete Book of Dried Arrangements by Raye Miller Underwood, 1952, M. Barrows & Co., Inc., New York.

Complete Book of Flowers and Plants for Interior Decoration by Esther Wheeler and Anabel Combs Lasker, 1957, Hearthside Press, Inc., New York.

Contemporary Flower Arrangement by Rae L. Goldson, 1955, Hearthside Press, Inc., New York.

Conway's Treasury of Flower Arrangement by J. Gregory Conway, 1953, Alfred J. Knopf, New York.

Design and Depth in Flower Arrangement by Emma Hodkinson Cyphers, 1958, Hearthside.

Flowers: East-West, by J. Gregory Conway, 1938, Alfred A. Knopf.

Flower Arranging for Fun by Hazel Peckinpaugh Dunlop, 1959, Studio-Viking.

Gardening, Forcing, Conditioning and Drying for Flower Arrangement by Arno and Irene Nehrling, 1958, Hearthside Press.

History of Flower Arrangement by Julia S. Berrall, 1953, Studio. Pub.

Holiday Flower Arrangement by Emma Hodkinson Cyphers, 1954, Hearthside Press.

Making Corsages at Home by Dorothy Biddle and Dorothea Blom, 1952, M. Barrows & Co. (out of print).*

Modern Art in Flower Arrangement by Emma Hodkinson Cyphers, 1959, Hearthside Press.

New Ways with Dried Flowers by Ruth Gannon, 1958, Studio Pub.

Period Flower Arrangement by Margaret Fairbanks Marcus, 1952, M. Barrows & Co.

Religious Themes in Flower Arrangement by Ruth E. Mullins, 1959, Hearthside Press.

The Art of Drying Plants and Flowers, by Mabel Squires, 1959.

The Art of Japanese Flower Arrangement by Alfred Koehn, 1933, Houghton-Mifflin Co. (out of print).*

The Magic World of Flower Arranging by Myra J. Brooks with Mary Alice and John P. Roche, 1956, M. Barrows & Co.

* Available in libraries.

SOURCES FOR ARRANGERS' SUPPLIES

Dorothy Biddle Service, Hawthorne, New York.
Floral Art, 26–28 Mason Street, Springfield, Massachusetts.
Flower Arrangers' Shop, 223 E. 58th Street, New York, New York.
Mrs. Robert Barton's Garden Shop, 75 Granite Street, Foxboro, Massachusetts.
Museum Pieces, Inc., 114 E. 32nd Street, New York, New York. (containers; statuary)

INDEX

(Numbers in italic indicate illustrations)